THE UNITY OF HOMER

THE UNITY OF HOMER

BY

JOHN A. SCOTT

BIBLO and TANNEN
NEW YORK
1965

Reprinted with the permission of
The University of California Press
Berkeley, Calif.

883
Sc08m
90301
oct/1974

BIBLO AND TANNEN
Booksellers and Publishers, Inc.
63 Fourth Avenue   New York, N.Y. 10003

Library of Congress Catalog Card Number: 65-15246

Printed in U.S.A. by
NOBLE OFFSET PRINTERS, INC.
NEW YORK 3, N. Y.

CONTENTS

CHAPTER I

HOMER AMONG THE ANCIENT GREEKS

The great fact of ancient Greece is the poetry of Homer, which was the center of education, the source of mythology, the model of literature, the inspiration of artists; known and quoted by all. Homer was a poet of such authority, even in matters not poetic, that contending states were supposed to have settled their claims to territory on the interpretation of his verses. Passing westward the power of Homeric verse transformed the Latin tongue, making the Romans abandon their own poetic forms and forcing that language, with its long case endings, to march in dactylic rhythms. The oldest Latin literature of which any fragments have been preserved is a version of the Odyssey, and the greatest poetic production of Roman Italy is the *Aeneid* of Vergil, a literary amalgamation and adaptation of both the Iliad and the Odyssey. Homer was thus in turn to inspire the genius of Dante; and the introduction of Milton's *Paradise Lost*, "Sing, heavenly Muse," shows the kinship of that poem also with Homeric poetry.

Nothing could better illustrate the preëminence of Homer than the fact that among the papyrus fragments discovered in Egypt four hundred and seventy are from the works of writers previously known, of which two hundred and seventy, far more than half, are from Homer. Demosthenes comes second with but thirty, and Plato, with only twenty, comes third.[1]

This popularity of Homer in Egypt is in keeping with the best opinion of classical Greece, for Plato, who reached manhood during the life of Sophocles and of Euripides, regarded Homer as the greatest of all the tragic poets; and oddly enough the genuine works of Plato contain hardly a verse from those mighty dramatists, although they are the most quotable of poets, while Homer is quoted more than one hundred times, many of these quotations containing several verses.[2] To the mind of the ancient world Homer stood quite alone, so that that great judge of literature, the Latin Quintilian, could say that Homer was to be approached by none and that it was a mark of ability to be able to appreciate him (x, 1, 50). Horace, whose own poetry is sufficient guaranty of his literary acumen, refers to Homer as the poet of perfect taste, *qui nil molitur inepte* (*Ars Poetica* 140).

This first and greatest of poets lives only in his poetry. In that poetry he tells us absolutely nothing about himself, his name, his home, his

[1] Kenyon, *Journal of Hellenic Studies*, 1919, 1 ff.

[2] Howes, ''Homeric Quotations in Plato and Aristotle,'' Harvard *Studies*, VI, 155. Aeschylus is quoted in *Rep.* II, 362 A; Euripides, in the spurious *Alcibiades* II, 151 B.

age, or his ancestors; and we can only surmise
his religious and political ideas as we read these
ideas into the actions or descriptions of the poems.

Homer was such a master of dramatic narrative that each character represents only himself.
When once Nestor, Achilles, Helen, Hector, or
Agamemnon has been brought into action, each
seems to live his own life, free to act or to speak
as he pleases, entirely detached from the mind
which created him.

The poet seems never to have made an allusion
to contemporary events, so that it is impossible
to assign him to a definite age; and his references
to rivers, mountains, lands, and seas are so im-
personal, so involved in the story he is telling,
that it is as difficult to name his home as it is to
define his time.

Not only does he name no contemporary
person or event, but he, too, is unnamed in any
contemporary source, so that practically every
statement made regarding him is due to the
creative imagination of those who had little or
nothing on which to build except inferences drawn
from the poems themselves. It is a significant
fact that different traditions in regard to Homer,
his life and his work, become fuller and more
definite as they get farther away from any possible sources of knowledge. My own belief is that
Homer was born in Smyrna, that he traveled much,
that the island of Chios was closely connected
with his life, also that he lived at approximately

900 B.C., or about one hundred years after David composed his *Songs,* and Solomon his *Proverbs.* The greatest period of Hebrew literature therefore would roughly correspond with the age of Homer.

The name of Smyrna is not mentioned by Homer, but the indications that this was his native city are as follows: The language in which these poems were composed is the Early Ionic with very marked survivals of Aeolic forms, a species of literary language which could hardly have responded to the thrill of creative genius except on the western shores of Asia Minor. The poet refers (B 535) to the men of Locris as living on the other side of Euboea, and since Locris is west of Euboea this must be viewed from the east. He speaks (B 145) of the waves being raised by the southwest winds or dashed by these same winds (B 395) against a jutting promontory, or of fogs forced landward by winds from the west (Δ 422), or of clouds driven on by Zephyrus moving over the deep (Δ 275), and of the mass of seaweeds washed ashore by gales from the north and west as these gales swept down from Thrace (I 5). In Homer the west wind, Zephyrus, is regularly a rough and disagreeable wind, while to most Greek and Latin writers it is the gentle and kindly breeze. Wood made the observation that only in the regions adjacent to Smyrna and along the Aegean coast of Asia Minor is the southwest wind a disagreeable one; while on the other shores of the Mediterranean it is especially the balmy Zephyrus.[3] Vergil's Latin feeling for this breeze did not permit him to follow Homer in making Zephyrus a rough and disagreeable wind. All these references imply a knowledge of the eastern shores of the Mediterranean, and the mention of the star of autumn (E 5) rising fresh from its bath in the ocean, and like references to the sun (H 422, T 1) would imply a view of the star or the sunrise such as the islands of the Aegean might supply.

The verses which furnish the most definite indication of the poet's nativity are those in which he describes the movements of the assembling hosts and the noises they make (B 459): "Just as the many flocks of winged birds, cranes, or geese, or long-necked swans in a meadow of Asia, about the streams of the Caÿster, fly here and there sporting on their pinions and alighting with loud cries, while the meadow reëchoes." This description of the lighting of birds seems based on the impression this sight must have made on the youthful mind of the poet, and we may safely assume that Homer had watched with boyish delight these flocks of geese, cranes, and swans as they settled in the valley of the Caÿster. The Caÿster was but a few miles from Smyrna, near enough to be known to a boy of that city, but still not too near to dull the impressions by the familiarity of frequent observance.

[3] *Essay on the Original Genius and Writings of Homer*, London, 1769.

Every person who is familiar with the life of the ancient Greeks knows what a high value they put upon fish as food, so high indeed that the word for dainty is also the word for the meat of fish, ὄψον. The gourmand and the spendthrift were persons who wasted their substance in buying fish of fine quality; yet in Homer the heroes spurned fish and the two passages which describe the eating of that food add the pardoning phrase, "for they were on the verge of starvation." (δ 369, μ 332.) The reason for this aversion to fish in Homer is very simple, and is as follows: Sir William Ramsay in his book, *Impressions of Turkey,* gives a closing chapter which he calls "Tips to Archaeologists," in which he describes upland trips from Smyrna. Sir William lays stress on the necessity of procuring proper food, especially meat, for such trips, and urges the traveler to rely on sardines to be taken along, or on kids and lambs to be obtained of the natives, but to avoid fish. His words in regard to fish are:

Fish are rarely found and when found are usually bad; the natives have a prejudice against fish, and my own experience has been unfavorable. Fish of considerable size swarm in the Tembris, but are flabby and taste like mud: two hungry archaeologists, after a mouthful or two of such a fish, could eat no more. In the clear, sparkling mountain stream that flows through the Taurus a small fish is caught; I had a most violent attack of sickness after eating some of them, and so had all who partook.

An educated native of Smyrna has assured me that fish from nearby streams are regarded by the natives with great disfavor and that this food is eaten only by the very poor. Evidently it was no accident that made Homer describe his heroes as abstaining from fish except under great compulsion, and we have in this a touch of local color and of local prejudice. It was because fish were in such disfavor as food in the neighborhood of Smyrna that the poet could not bring himself to serve them to his mighty warriors.[4]

All the lines by which Homeric poetry traveled to the outer world converged at the central and western coast of Asia Minor. Hence came the bards who recited Homer and hence originated the colonies, such as Sinope and Marseilles, which furnished manuscripts for the scholars of Alexandria. Cynaethus, also, is said to have taken the knowledge of Homer from Chios to Sicily, and Lycurgus that same knowledge from Samos to Sparta.

Finally, Smyrna is easily the preferred city in all the lives of Homer and among all the traditions of those who laid claim to his place of birth; also the poet was called by a second name, Melesigenes, from the river Melas, near or in Smyrna. Whether he was thus called because he was regarded as the child of the river or from some festival held on its banks cannot now be determined.

The language employed, the indications of the poem, the radiation of the knowledge of the poetry

[4] "Homeric Heroes and Fish," *Classical Journal*, XII, 328.

from the west and central coast of Asia Minor, the antipathy to fish as food, the fair agreement of tradition, and the name Melesigenes, all unite in warranting the belief that the poetry of Homer originated in the neighborhood of Smyrna. The island of Chios, long a favored spot for the preservation of his poetry, was the home of a guild of singers who called themselves the Homeridae. We do not know whether they claimed to be the descendants or the successors of Homer, but it is probable that they regarded themselves as peculiarly the defenders and interpreters of the poet whose name they had assumed.

The earliest conjecture we have regarding the date of Homer is found in Herodotus (ii, 53), where, in contrasting the great antiquity of Egypt with the recent civilization of Greece, the historian says that he would not assign to Homer an earlier date than four hundred years before his own time, and this opinion he has not derived from others, but it is his own conclusion. Since Herodotus flourished in the middle of the fifth century before Christ his estimate would put Homer in the middle of the ninth century, a time in Greek civilization which has left surprisingly few evidences on which to make a conjecture. How important the independent opinion of Herodotus is we may judge from the fact that even this estimate assigns Homer to an age as remote from his own as Columbus is from our times.

The matters in the poem on which to base inferences in regard to the poet's date are extremely slight. The Odyssey (ω 89) describes the wrestlers as girding up their loins. But we know that wrestlers dispensed with the girdle at the fifteenth Olympiad; hence the presumption that this verse is older than 720. The poet in speaking of Phoenicia never mentions Tyre or the Tyrians, but only Sidon and the Sidonians. Sidon was completely overthrown in 677, leaving Tyre as the sole heir to the greatness of Phoenicia, so that in the use of the words Sidon and Sidonians we can say no more than that Homer was describing a condition which terminated in 677 B.C.[5] The fact that Lydia is called only by the older name Maeonia gives no clue to the date, for we do not know when the name was changed to Lydia. Even if we knew definitely it must be remembered that Homer is a poet and that he might have used the old name even after the new name had come into general use, just as Milton refers to Alexander as the Emathian conqueror at a time when Macedonia was universally known, and Emathia only a learned survival. On the other hand Homer speaks of the men who fought at Troy as belonging to a race greatly superior to those of his own day. But even here his references are so vague that many early and some late scholars would make Homer a contemporary with the events he describes.

[5] "Sidon and the Sidonians in Homer," *Class. Jour.*, XIV, 525.

The discoveries made at Troy, Mycenae, and elsewhere suffice to show that Troy was destroyed during the twelfth century, so that Homer must be subsequent to that event. The Iliad and the Odyssey seem to have been known to Hesiod, who quoted them, changed or corrected them, but never mentioned their names or the name of their author. Hesiod can hardly be put later than the middle of the eighth century. Terpander is said to have won, about 675 B.C., a victory in a musical contest in which he set to new music the words of Homer; and the Iliad and the Odyssey seem to furnish the background or the starting point for that mass of tradition which was put in verse during the early Olympiads.

However much Homer may have influenced the poetry of the ages immediately succeeding his own, it is a remarkable fact that no mention of his name by any writer before the latter half of the sixth century has been preserved, and even that mention owes its preservation to writers living after Christ, who quoted it in their own works. The first known reference is found in a fragment of Xenophanes from Colophon, who censured Homer for the ignoble traits he assigned to the gods. The language used by Xenophanes argues for great antiquity of the poetry of Homer, especially the phrase: "From the beginning, according to Homer, for all have learned from him." This first preserved reference to Homer is hardly older than 550, while the Iliad and the

Odyssey are first referred to by name in the writings of Herodotus, or about one hundred years after Xenophanes.

The night which surrounds Homer is thus both long and dark, but more wonderful than these silences is the fact that these two great poems have come down to us entire. No gaps are found in either, no incomplete lines, no half-preserved sentences. Not a single ancient writer has alluded to a single scene of the Iliad or the Odyssey which is not found in the present text of these poems, even if certain random verses have been preserved which are not in the Vulgate.

What the preservation of poems so ancient and so bulky signifies may be grasped by the fact that many early epics, such as the *Thebais,* the *Cypria,* the *Little Iliad,* the *Destruction of Troy,* the *Nostoi,* poems of the Epic Cycle, have been entirely lost, or preserved merely by chance quotations or references in late authors. The advanced critics of Homer, however, such as Verrall, Murray, and Wilamowitz, would draw no distinction between the Iliad, the Odyssey and these lost poems; they assign them all to the same source. Verrall in an article published in the *Quarterly Review* for July, 1908 said: "Homer, so-called, is a nebulous mass of old poetry reduced into distinct bodies, such as *Iliad, Odyssey, Cypria, Aethiopis, Little Iliad, Nostoi,* and so forth for educational purposes by learned Athenians, about 600–500 B.C." Murray in his *Rise of the Greek Epic* tries to prove that all the early epics were the slow growth of centuries, the work of numberless bards. On page 200 he says: "The truth is that all these poems or masses of tradition in verse form were growing up side by side for centuries." Wilamowitz constantly argues that at the beginning of the fifth century all epic poetry was assigned to Homer, and even so clear a thinker as Andrew Lang agreed with that opinion, for in a lecture published in *Anthropology and the Classics* he said: "To Homer early historic Greece attributed the great body of ancient epic poetry."

If these statements be true and early Greece did regard all this vast cycle as of common origin and of equal merit, then little remains to be said in regard to Homer, the man, the creator of the Iliad and the Odyssey, since so many and so bulky poems could never have originated with any one man, but must have been the work of guilds or schools coöperating through many ages. A discussion of the assumed ancient belief that Homer was the author of all these poems deserves first consideration in any comprehensive treatment of the Homeric Question.

There is not a writer before the death of Aristotle who quotes, naming the poem, a single verse from any of these poems, except the Iliad and the Odyssey, as the work of Homer; not one who writes "As Homer said in the *Thebais,* the *Cypria,* or the *Little Iliad.*" Writers of the best

period frequently quote the Iliad or the Odyssey
with the introductory words "as Homer says in
the Iliad," or "as Homer says in the Odyssey,"
and the common method in early writers or grammarians is to refer to the poems of the Epic Cycle
thus: "as the writer of the *Cypria* says," or "as
the poet of the *Little Iliad* wrote," and so with
all the Cycle; but I have never seen an early
example of such indefinite phrases used concerning the Iliad and the Odyssey. As already stated,
the regular form is "as Homer says in the Iliad,"
or "as Homer says in the Odyssey." The authorship of these two poems is never referred to some
indefinite poet or source.

Every argument which is used to prove the
Homeric authorship of the Cycle—and by the
Cycle I mean the poetry connected with Thebes
and Troy other than the Iliad and the Odyssey—
and all the quotations are either from very late
writers, or from the lost works of early writers,
fragments accidentally preserved and out of their
context, where the meaning is largely a matter
of interpretation, conjecture, or emendation. All
these indirect references are to be treated with
the greatest caution, and no unsupported quotation from any writer, however good or early that
writer may be, is to be regarded as absolutely
conclusive.

Literary references by modern writers are
often notoriously inaccurate; for example, in the
American Magazine for January, 1920 a list of

questions is asked, the ability to answer which is to be regarded as the mark of a broad education. One of these questions is, "For what is Sheridan famous?" On a later page the answer is given, "Sheridan wrote 'She Stoops to Conquer.'" The man who wrote that question and answer was probably sitting in a room which contained the works both of Sheridan and of Goldsmith, yet if that same writer had lived two thousand years ago such a statement would be regarded as final proof. It is impossible to exaggerate the mass of false references in our modern journals, or the number of quotations falsely assigned to Shakespeare and the Bible. The scarcity and the expense of books in early ages must have made accurate quotation far more difficult then than now. Plutarch, Aelian, and Athenaeus, three of our chief sources for references to older writers, are woefully inexact, as any competent reader of these learned men knows; and Plato in two places quotes the same verse from Hesiod, but in different ways. He repeatedly gives parts of two verses as if they were a single verse, and he also has a jumbled form of perfectly good verses, while in the spurious *Theages* (125B) there is quoted as if from Euripides a verse which on excellent authority is assigned to Sophocles. Aristotle, the most learned man of antiquity, quotes the words of Odysseus (μ 219) as the words of Calypso (*Ethics* ιι, 9, 3); also he repeats the speech of Agamemnon (B 393) as if spoken by Hector (*Ethics* III, 11, 4), and in his *Rhetoric* (III, 9, p. 1409 b 8) he assigns a verse of Euripides to Sophocles. Aristophanes (*Birds* 575) substitutes Iris for Hera in quoting Iliad E 778. The scholia often assign verses to Homer which are in the extant works of other writers, e.g. the scholium to Pindar (*O.* XIII, 12) credits Homer with a verse which is found in the poetry of Theognis, and another scholium to Pindar (*N.* VI, 91) quotes Homer as the source of a verse which is found in Hesiod. The outstanding importance of Homer made him a sort of universal source for all kinds of verses. This must never be forgotten in estimating the importance of various quotations. In view of these undoubted errors in primary and secondary sources we cannot accept quotations made by late and inaccurate writers as final evidence of authorship, unless that evidence is definite, unequivocal, and confirmed by reliable testimony.

The inferences that Homer was early regarded as the author of the Epic Cycle are as follows: The *Thebais*,[6] an assumed poem dealing with the Argive expedition against Thebes, is said by Wilamowitz, Finsler, and many others to be the first poem to be definitely assigned to Homer. This first reference to Homer was made by Callinus, an elegiac poet, who lived in Ephesus early in the seventh century before Christ. The source of this statement is a sentence in Pausanias IX, 9, 5.

6 "Homer as the Poet of the *Thebais*," *Classical Philology*, XVI, 20 ff.

"The epic poem, the *Thebais*, was written in regard to this war, and Calaenus, when he speaks of this poem, said that he regarded the author as Homer. [It may also be translated, he regarded the author as an Homer.] Many others agree with Calaenus in this, but while I praise this poem I yet put it after the Iliad and the Odyssey." It seems that all that this passage is intended to show is the high estimate in which the *Thebais* was held and that even here the author of that poem is regarded as an equal with the great Homer. Not a manuscript has the word Callinus in this place, but all have Calaenus, so that Callinus is simply an emendation. The word Callinus is a pure conjecture; but even if all the manuscripts had the form Callinus, it would be more than doubtful if the poet of Ephesus was intended, for that early poet was so little known that his name is not mentioned until Strabo, and when Strabo mentions the name he adds the phrase, "the poet of the elegy" (xiii, 604); and when he refers to him a little later he again adds the words "the poet of the elegy" (xiii, 627). The repetition of the phrase shows that the mere mention of his name could not be regarded as a sufficient indication of the person intended.

Pausanias just a little earlier (viii, 25, 4) has said that the story of the expedition against Thebes had been put into verse by Antimachus, who was at the time of Pausanias one of the most popular of all the Greek poets, and Dio Cassius

(LXIX, 4) is the authority for the statement that Hadrian esteemed Antimachus and his *Thebais* more highly than the poetry of Homer. Kinkel gives fifty-six fragments from this *Thebais* of Antimachus, while he has but seven from the earlier poem, most of which are doubtful.

The earlier fragments are so few, while those from the poem by Antimachus are so many, that the mere mention of the name *Thebais* is almost certain to refer to the poem by Antimachus; but here there can be no reasonable doubt, since Pausanias (VIII, 25, 4) says he is referring to that poem. Hadrian put Antimachus ahead of Homer, Calaenus made him the equal, and Pausanias, even if he appreciated the greatness of the *Thebais* of Antimachus, put him just behind Homer. Paley, in his *Homeri Quae Nunc Extant* etc., p. 39, argued that the Antimachus of the *Thebais* was really the poet of the Iliad and the Odyssey. There is nothing in Pausanias to show that he is not referring to Antimachus; the reading is not Callinus, but Calaenus. And even if the reading were Callinus, there is nothing to connect him with the poet of Ephesus; yet this is the sole evidence for the assertion that Homer was regarded in the seventh century B.C. as the poet of the *Thebais*.

The second writer quoted to prove that Homer was regarded as the author of the *Thebais* is Herodotus, from whom the following passage is cited: "The tyrant of Sicyon, Cleisthenes, when

he was at war with Argos, banished the Homeric
bards because the poetry of Homer so constantly
praised Argos and the Argives.'' (v, 67.)

Grote, *History of Greece,* II, 174, argued that
it must have been the *Thebais* which so angered
Cleisthenes, and Wilamowitz followed him by saying (*H. U.* 352): ''This can make sense here only
if Homer is regarded as the poet of the *Thebais.*''
Finsler accepts this as an established fact, saying
in his *Homer,* I, 64: ''The *Thebais* is meant, when
the tyrant, Cleisthenes, banished the bards from
Sicyon, since the Homeric poetry gave too little
honor to Argos.'' That is, they all assume that
there is not enough praise of the Argives in the
Iliad and the Odyssey to arouse either the pride
of the men of Argos or the envy of their hostile
neighbors; hence they fly to an assumed *Thebais,*
the contents of which are also assumed. The
Argives or Argos are named in every book of the
Iliad except book twenty, and, despite the fact that
the Odyssey withdraws to Ithaca or to fairyland,
they are named in fifteen books of that poem;
hence they are named in thirty-eight books of
our Homer. Hera is ''Argive Hera,'' Helen is
''Argive Helen,'' and Agamemnon with his divine
scepter ruled over ''many isles and all Argos.''
Rawlinson, with no thought of this discussion,
says in his note to the first chapter of his *Herodotus:* ''The ancient superiority of Argos is indi-
cated by the position of Agamemnon at the time
of the Trojan War and by the use of Argive in

Homer for Greek generally. No other name of a single people is used in the same generic way.'' Here this competent historian bases the claim for Argive superiority entirely on the campaign before Troy, that is, on the Iliad and the Odyssey.

However, this is not a question of probabilities, for we know from the men of Argos themselves the poetry which stirred their pride, since we have a copy of the very inscription they set up in honor of Homer. This inscription is added to the *Contest between Homer and Hesiod* as published in the works of Hesiod. The account of the inscription and the inscription itself is as follows:

The leaders of Argos rejoicing greatly in the fact that their own people have been so highly honored by the most illustrious of poets have in turn loaded him with conspicuous honors. They erected a bronze image and voted him a sacrifice for each day, each month, each year, and in addition every fifth year sent an offering for his glory to Chios. On his image they engraved the following verses: ''This is divine Homer, who adorned all proud Hellas with his wonderful poetic skill but most of all he honored the Argives, who humbled the god-built city Troy, as a requital for the wrongs done to the fair-haired Helen, and hence the proud-citied state worships him with divine honors.''

Thus we have from the Argives themselves the thing in Homer which they viewed with such boundless pride, and this was no exploit connected with Thebes: it was the expedition against Troy; that is, they felt exalted because Homer had honored them in the Iliad and the Odyssey

Thebes is not mentioned in the inscription. There can be no doubt that hostile neighbors would envy them that very thing in which they themselves took such unbounded pride. The story of this expedition is found in no assumed *Thebais,* but in Homer, our Homer, the Homer of the Iliad and the Odyssey.

Inasmuch as Thebes went over to the Persians it would seem natural for the Argives to stress their old conflicts at the time of the Persian War, but oddly enough the Argives never lay claim to honor or favor because of those early exploits. Yet the Athenians at the battle of Plataea claimed as one of the reasons for commanding the wing not held by the Spartans their own services at that time, and they said (*Her.* ix, 27) : "When the Argives led their troops with Polynices against Thebes and were slain and refused burial, it is our boast that we went out against the Cad-maeans, recovered the bodies and buried them at Eleusis in our own territory." In the face of this the critics assume that there was nothing in the Iliad and the Odyssey to stir the pride of the Argives or to arouse the envy of jealous neigh-bors; accordingly they flee to a poem which told how these same Argives could not bury their own slain but depended on the mercies of a foreign race to bury them in a foreign soil. The love the people of Argos had for Homer is also shown by the fact that Aristarchus quoted readings from the Argive state manuscript of both the Iliad and the Odyssey, but there is not the slightest evidence that they made any attempt to preserve a copy of the *Thebais*.

The third proof offered for the Homeric authorship of the *Thebais* is founded on the *Paradoxes* of Antigonus of Carystus, chap. 25, in which a reference is made to the nature of the polyp. The quotation is introduced with the words, ''As the poet has written in the much quoted verses.'' There is nothing to connect this either with Homer or the *Thebais* except the fact that the author is referred to by the phrase, ''the poet,'' ὁ ποιητής,—a phrase often used of Homer. The reason that Homer more than anyone else is called the poet is simply because he is quoted more than any other. But he has no vested right in these words. Plato in the *Laws* (901 A) refers to Hesiod with the unmodified words ''the poet,'' ὁ ποιητής, and we know that Hesiod is the one thus designated, since an extant poem of that author is quoted. There is not the slightest evidence that Antigonus had Homer in mind as the author of these verses. But the fact that Hesiod has been quoted only a few verses previously, and his well-known references to the polyp, make it probable that Hesiod was the author of this passage. These three references, one in Herodotus, one in Antigonus, and one in Pausanias, all based on unsupported and improbable conjectures, are the only evidence presented to show that the Greeks of the best period assigned the *Thebais* to Homer;

yet if one reads Wilamowitz' latest book on Homer he is made to feel that Homer's earliest and greatest reputation is closely connected with this hypothetical *Thebais*.

In the *Panegyricus* 158, Isocrates tells of the sadness the Greeks always feel when told of the wars between the Greeks. Then he adds: ''I think that the poetry of Homer has received the greater glory because he pictures them as fighting foreigners, and it was just because of this that our ancestors honored him in musical festivals and in the education of the young.'' Since the Argive expedition was a war between Greeks, this remark of Isocrates would have been absurd if Homer were regarded as the poet of the *Thebais,* or if there had been any such tradition. This speech of Isocrates was no random production but a piece of literary display on which he had spent long and careful labor, and is a far better criterion for the beliefs of his own and the preceding generation than the random remark, conjectural remark at that, of writers coming several centuries later. Homer is definitely connected with the *Thebais* in the *Contest between Homer and Hesiod,* but, since this contains the name of the Emperor Hadrian, it must be regarded as a late production.

The Cyclic poem from which there are preserved the most verses is the *Cypria,* the poem which tells of the choice of Paris, the rape of Helen, and in general the events connected with

the Trojan War as far as the beginning of the
Iliad. Most of the references assign this poem to
Stasinus, or they leave the author unnamed and
ambiguous, as "the one who created the *Cypria*,"
ὁ τὰ Κύπρια πεποιηκώς, ὁ τὰ Κύπρια ποιήσας, or "the
poet of the *Cypria*," ὁ τῶν Κυπρίων ποιητής. The
extant works of but two early writers, Herodotus
and Plato, quote the *Cypria*. In Herodotus there
is not even a quotation, only a loose paraphrase.

Herodotus II, 117 contrasts the direct and easy
voyage which took Helen to Troy as told in the
Cypria with the circuitous journey described in
the Iliad, and hence, he said, the *Cypria* could not
be the work of Homer. This is the only direct
reference in classical Greek to Homer as the poet
of the *Cypria*, and this reference is a denial of
that poem to Homer. Wilamowitz jumps from
this to the conclusion that here is the first doubt
cast on Homer's title to all the Cycle. He sees
in Herodotus a Luther at the Diet of Worms, who
dared defy the universal opinion of society, and
accordingly draws the inference that up to that
time no one had ever questioned the Homeric
authorship of the entire mass of early epic poetry.
He is referred to as the direct ancestor of Wolf;
and just as Wolf dared assert that Homer was
not the author of all the Iliad, so Herodotus dared
proclaim that the Cycle was not all by Homer.

The life of Herodotus was exactly contemporary with the rise of the Sophists. Protagoras,
who was the first to give himself that name, was

born in a neighboring town within a few years of
the birth of Herodotus. The Sophists prided
themselves on their ability to prove either side of
any question, and even Socrates was accused of
taking the worse side and making it appear the
better. We have, under the famous name of
Gorgias, an essay or speech illustrating how
sophistic skill can take the faults of Helen and
make of them a garland of virtues; and in the writings of Antiphon we have a series of speeches in
which it is shown how the same facts may be used
as evidence for exactly opposite arguments. No
doubt a common theme for these sophistic exercises would be the question of authorship of poems
of doubtful or unknown origin. This would give
abundant opportunity for paradoxical argumen-
tative skill. Herodotus may well be replying to
an argument of this sort by calling attention to
something which had been overlooked. Recently
a modern sophist has written a long treatise for
the purpose of proving that the works of Shakespeare were written by the Earl of Oxford, just
as other earlier sophists tried to prove that they
were written by Bacon. If a modern writer should
call attention to some point or fact that made
impossible either of these theories, would that be
accepted as proof that this scholar stood alone in
denying a common belief? In the age when the
faith of all believed in a single Homer, Aristarchus
made many comments in support of that belief.
We know that these comments were directed

against the paradoxes of Xenon, and that it was
not Aristarchus but Xenon who was attacking the
common belief. We can assume that Herodotus
took a like position and that he, as well as Aristarchus, supported the accepted beliefs against
the sophistic vagaries. The passage in which
Herodotus furnishes proof that the *Cypria* cannot
be by Homer is the main support for the theory
that Homer was regarded as the author of that
poem.

The *Cypria* is quoted by Plato in the
Euthyphro 12 A in a manner which shows that
he did not assign it to Homer, as the phrase
ὁ ποιητὴς ἐποίησεν ὁ ποιήσας is most vague and indefinite. Aelian is sometimes cited to prove that
Pindar regarded Homer as the author of the
Cypria. The passage in Aelian (*Var. Hist.* IX, 15)
is as follows:

> The Argives assign to Homer the first place in poetry
> and regarded all others as second to him. They sacrifice
> to him, inviting Apollo and Homer. This also is said,
> that, being without resources to dower his daughter, he
> gave her as a present the *Cypria*. Pindar also agrees
> in this.

καὶ ὁμολογεῖ τοῦτο Πίνδαρος. To what does Pindar
agree, the preëminence of Homer, or that he gave
his daughter the *Cypria* as a dowry? It is very
hard to decide, since we have no inkling of the
context or of the thing which Pindar was intend-
ing to say. Aelian in this passage is unusually
obscure, and even when his meaning is perfectly
definite he is so unreliable that we are rarely

certain either of the matter or the person quoted.
This applies to all his writings and most of all
to his *Varia Historia* from which this quotation
is taken, since it has been preserved only in ex-
tracts and the original was culled from the works
of men many of whom were as little to be trusted
as Aelian himself. We seem to be forcing even
this unreliable witness, when we quote him as
saying that Pindar regarded Homer as the author
of the *Cypria*.

A late age which ignorantly referred all early
poetry to Homer was forced to explain the fact
that most of these poems were regarded as the
works of other poets, and so took refuge in the
assumption that, even if these poems were not
credited to Homer, he had composed them and
then waived his rights therein by presenting them
to the poet who had married his daughter, or that
he had bartered them for sustenance to the men
under whose names they had circulated. These
tales are no proof that Homer was regarded as
the source of these various poems, but just the
reverse; they show that they were regarded as
the creations of the various poets whose names
they bore. Thus was provided an easy explanation for the fact that the names of Arctinus,
Stasinus, and the rest were attached to these
poems, although all the early epics must have been
the work of Homer.

Perhaps the sentence most quoted to prove
that Homer was regarded as the author of the

Epic Cycle is the one in which Aeschylus is reported to have said that his own plays were but
portions from the great Homeric banquet. Since
very few of the plays of Aeschylus touch the
traditions given in the Iliad and the Odyssey, the
assumption has been generally made that a wider
meaning must be given to the word Homer than
merely the poet of these two poems. The passage
is found in Athenaeus VIII, 347 E:

Ulpianus seems to eat nothing befitting a man, but
to watch those eating to see if they overlook a bit of bone,
of gristle, or of cartilage from the pieces served, not
heeding the words of the noble and illustrious Aeschylus,
who said that his own dramas were portions from
Homer's great feasts.

ὃς τὰς αὑτοῦ τραγῳδίας τεμάχη εἶναι ἔλεγε τῶν Ὁμήρου
μεγάλων δείπνων. Even those who interpret this as
the statement of the poet that he took his plays
from Homer find it difficult to explain how the
Persians, the *Prometheus Bound,* the *Hiketides,*
could have thus originated. Those who try to
render τεμάχη by crumbs or scraps miss the meaning entirely, for the word means portions or slices
of fish, the choicest of Athenian foods (Phrynichus
XIII τὸ δὲ τέμαχος μόνον ἐπὶ ἰχθύος). Rutherford in
a note to this definition gives a long list of quotations to show that this word denotes the best and
most coveted of courses. The words in Athenaeus
which immediately follow, "Aeschylus, even when
defeated in a dramatic contest, proudly said that
he left the decision to time, since he knew that he
would receive his merited honors," show that the

poet was not speaking in humility but in pride, and that he is not represented as comparing his tragedies to crumbs from the Homeric banquets, but to whole courses or portions which were left uneaten, or as the poet calls them τεμάχη.

The meaning then is that some small-minded fellow sat searching for neglected scraps which the feasters rejected or overlooked, while Aeschylus was able to secure whole portions of the choicest viands from the banquet set before Homer. It was the good luck of Aeschylus that the Homeric banquet was so lavish that he was not reduced to crumbs but could feast on whole courses which the earlier poet did not use. If one will read the context in Athenaeus which just precedes and immediately follows the quotation from Aeschylus, he will see that the poet is not speaking in self-depreciation[7] but exultation. No good Greek ever spoke with false humility of his own work—Uriah Heep was not a native of Attica. This interpretation makes impossible the presumption that Aeschylus regarded Homer as the poet of the entire Cycle. Pindar refers to Homer by name several times, each time a free adaptation of our present Homer, just the adaptation needed to change the epic meter and dialect into the lyric strains and dialect of Pindar. Aristophanes in the extant plays refers to Homer or quotes him six times, either in an exact quota-

[7] The bearing of the boast of Aeschylus, that "he left the decision in regard to his tragedies to the verdict of time," was pointed out to me by Professor Ivan M. Linforth.

tion or in such a way as to show that he is
referring to the Iliad and the Odyssey.. In a fragment of the earliest play of this comic poet an
old man questions a youth on the meaning of two
obscure Homeric words, both of which are in our
present text of Homer.

Athenaeus (IV 172 E), says that in a poem of
Simonides the following verses are used in regard
to Meleager: "Who surpassed all young men in
the use of the spear, hurling it over the eddying
Anaurus from Iolcus, rich in vines. Thus Homer
and Stesichorus sang to their people." This quotation is so indefinite, so out of all connection
and context, that it is rash to hazard an interpretation. The meaning might be clear if the quotation were longer. We know that in the story of
the ninth book of the Iliad, Phoenix tried to impress Achilles with horror of the ruin wrought
by the unyielding attitude of Meleager. This
obstinacy of Meleager may be the thing to which
reference is here made, but the fragment is too
brief to give any indication of the use to which
the tradition was applied. The fragment is purely
negative and yields nothing on which to build
theories of contents or of authorship.

The last proof which I shall quote from
classical writers that Homer was regarded as the
poet of the Epic Cycle is furnished by the speech
of Aeschines against Timarchus (128 ff.), a speech
delivered in 345 B.C., that is, after the death of
both Xenophon and Plato and during the prime

of Aristotle. In this speech the orator said that
Homer, in the Iliad, before anything happened,
often used the phrase ''rumor came to the army,''
Φήμη δ᾽ εἰς στρατὸν ἦλθε. These exact words are
not found in the present Iliad. The assumption
has therefore been made that Aeschines must have
meant the *Little Iliad;* and since the contents of
that poem are almost unknown it is easy to suppose that it had many examples of that phrase.
Homer does not use the word φήμη in this phrase,
but does have the exact synonym, the highly poetic
ὄσσα, in several passages, where the meaning is
essentially the same as that given by Aeschines:

B 93:   μετὰ δέ σφιν ὄσσα δεδήειν
          ὀτρύνουσ᾽ ἰέναι, Διὸς ἄγγελος.

ω 413: ὄσσα δ᾽ ἄρ᾽ ἄγγελος ὦκα κατὰ πτόλιν
          ᾤχετο πάντη.

So also in α 282, β 216. In all these sentences the
mysterious ὄσσα is used in exactly the same sense
as the φήμη of Aeschines, and it is as unreasonable
to look elsewhere for the origin of the phrase used
by the orator as it would be to seek for some other
source than Bishop Berkeley for the common
quotation, ''Westward the star of empire takes
its way,'' although he really said ''Westward the
course of empire takes its way.'' Thus all the
difference between Homer and Aeschines is that
the orator substituted the prose φήμη for the
highly poetic ὄσσα.

The evidence which I have presented is substantially all that can be gleaned from all the

writers before the death of Aristotle to show that
Homer was regarded until the middle of the fifth
century as the poet of the great mass of early
epic poetry. Not one clear and definite proof can
be found; each is weak, improbable, and dependent
on forced interpretations or forced conjectures
and emendations.

The reasons for believing that the Greeks of
the best period did not regard Homer as the
author of the Trojan and Theban Cycle are
definite and numerous:

1. Not a single writer of the best period quotes
a single verse as Homeric from the entire Cycle;
not one example of, for instance, "Homer says in
the *Thebais*," "Homer says in the *Cypria*"; while
hundreds of verses are quoted from the Iliad and
the Odyssey as the words of Homer.

2. A young man who is one of the speakers in
Xenophon's *Symposium* (III, 5), the scene of which
is laid at about 420 B.C., says: "My father, eager
to have me become a good man, compelled me to
commit to memory all the poetry of Homer, and
thus it happens that, even now, I can repeat from
memory all the Iliad and the Odyssey." Here the
words, "all the poetry of Homer," and "the Iliad
and the Odyssey," are interchangeable terms.
Antisthenes replies to the young man that this is
no great accomplishment, since all the rhapsodists
know all these poems, too. Not a man in that
group, not even the captious Socrates, suggested
that in using the phrase, "all the poetry of

Homer," he must remember that other poems than the Iliad and the Odyssey have been assigned to Homer. Xenophon is the best possible authority. He is early, is acquainted with many lands, a man of the world as well as a man of letters. He gives us the unequivocal statement that in his time among educated Athenians Homeric poetry was regarded as coëxtensive with the Iliad and the Odyssey.

(3.) An easy proof that the Greeks of the best period never regarded Homer as the author of the Cycle is found in the fact that Homer was to them the ideal of the best in poetry, to approach him was the highest praise any work of genius could receive, and the poetry of the Cycle was generally despised and neglected. A measure of the high esteem felt for the Iliad and the Odyssey and the low regard in which the Cycle was held is found in the fact that the Iliad and the Odyssey, despite their great length, have come down to us entire, and, even if they had been lost, quotations therefrom and references thereto are so many and so full that we could reconstruct their general outline from the material thus furnished, while the poems of the Cycle are so utterly and completely lost that we depend on a brief late prose summary for practically all our knowledge of them. Not a single line of some of them has been preserved, and Kinkel and Allen, in their full and exhaustive collection of the fragments, can not produce ten verses from all the Cycle which are found in the works of writers who lived before the death of Aristotle. It is a startling proof of the different regard in which the Iliad, the Odyssey, and the Epic Cycle were held that, according to Kenyon, in the fragments of known classical writers discovered in Egypt, far more than half of the total are from the Iliad and the Odyssey, while not a trace of the Cyclic poems has been found. Allen publishes one doubtful cyclic papyrus fragment.

The reason for the neglect of these poems in Greece and in Egypt is found in their small poetic merit and in their general lack of constructive ability. As proofs of this I shall furnish only five, but important, witnesses. Proclus, to whom we are indebted for most of our scanty knowledge of the Cycle, says, ''The poems of the Cycle were not preserved for their poetic merit, but because of the traditions and the mythology they contained.'' Horace, who, although a Roman poet, is earlier than much of the learned literature of the Greeks, says of Homer that he is the poet of perfect taste, *qui nil molitur inepte,* but he nevertheless holds up to ridicule the creative futility of the Cyclic poets and contrasts that futility with the unerring judgment of Homer. Callimachus, the learned librarian of Alexandria, refers to Homer as the ''divine Homer'' (*Ep.* 61), but he also says ''I hate the cyclic poem.''[8] (*Ep.* 29.)

8 Ludwich, *De Cyclo Homerico* (Königsberg, 1905), suggests that Callimachus may be referring here to an arrangement of words, such as appeared on the tomb of Midas, which is discussed

Important as these witnesses are in regard to the comparative merits of the Iliad, the Odyssey, and the Cycle, they are as nothing, since we have the testimony of Aristotle, a man who had the literature before him and who had the ability to appreciate it. In all his writings on poetry Aristotle regarded Homer as quite alone, the perfect example of taste, invention, and of execution. In his discussion of the unity of plot (*Poetics* VIII) he says: "Homer evidently understood that point perfectly, whether by art or by instinct, in exactly the same way that he excels the rest in every respect." By "the rest" he means the poets of the Epic Cycle, and again he says (*Poetics* XXIII): "Here then the transcendent excellence of Homer is manifest. He never attempts to make the whole war of Troy the subject of his poem, although that war had a beginning, a middle, and an end. All other poets took a single period, a single hero, or a single action indeed, but with a multiplicity of parts. Thus did the author of the *Cypria* and of the *Little Iliad*." Similar ideas abound in the works of Aristotle, that the Iliad and the Odyssey

in Plato's *Phaedrus* 264 D, and that he is not considering the Epic Cycle. The words of Proclus, οἱ μέντοι γ᾽ ἀρχαῖοι καὶ τὸν Κύκλον ἀναφέρουσιν εἰς αὐτόν, which are generally made the starting point for the assumption of Homeric authorship of the Cycle and are the first authority thus quoted by Christ-Schmid, are explained by Ludwich as having no sort of connection with the Epic Cycle, but simply referring to the word-play as given in the *Phaedrus*. Just as Homer was regarded as the father of oratory and tragedy, so to him was referred the creation of this play on words. This interpretation removes much of the evidence for the theory that Homer was early credited with the authorship of the Epic Cycle.

show exactly the same high poetic skill, the same
perfect control of plot, and in all these matters
stand alone and apart from all the poems of
the Epic Cycle.   And in the *Panathenaicus* of
Isocrates (XII, 263), an assumed speaker says of a
certain group of literary productions that "They
are as inferior to the work of Isocrates as those
were inferior to Homer who attempted like themes
with those put in verse by that great poet."
From these primary proofs it is evident that
the Iliad and the Odyssey were totally unlike all
the other poems of the Cycle.   Yet in the face of
such conclusive evidence we are calmly assured
that all these poems, the Iliad, the Odyssey, the
Thebais, the *Cypria,* and all the Cycle were simply
parts of a like mass of poetry, all bearing the
same marks and all assigned to the same poet,
Homer.   I am, however, unable to find any clear
and conclusive evidence that a single writer before the death of Aristotle assigned any poem
of the Cycle to Homer, or to find any suspicion
cast on the Homeric authorship of the Iliad and
the Odyssey.

It is worth the while to set over against everything that has been written on the Epic Cycle
from Welcker to Wilamowitz these two sentences:
"My father had me commit to memory all the
poetry of Homer and I can now repeat by heart
all the Iliad and the Odyssey," and "Homer,
admirable as he is in every other respect, is
especially so in this, that he alone among the epic

poets is not unaware of the part to be played by the poet himself in the poem." (Xen. *Sym.* III, 5, Aristotle *Poetics* XXIV.) These two passages do not need to be emended and they need no exegesis; hence they give no proper sphere for imaginative and creative scholarship. But they satisfy me and convince me that Homeric studies have no need to build on airy speculations when they have as a foundation such solid and unequivocal facts.

The assumption of most critics has been that in the early literary ages of Greece Homer was a general name to which was assigned the entire mass of early epic poetry, and that slowly first one poem was taken from him and then another until all but the Iliad and the Odyssey had been denied him, when a period of credulity followed that lasted until Wolf took up the work which had so long lain dormant. Wolf then is a kindred spirit with the great literary leaders of the Age of Pericles. The exact reverse, however, is the true story, for not a single verse, not a single poem of the Epic Cycle was definitely quoted as the work of Homer until after the death of Aristotle. The few verses gathered by Allen under the heading *Versus Heroici,* which are assigned to Homer and yet are not in the Iliad or the Odyssey, are adaptations or misquotations of verses in the Vulgate. It cannot be too strongly emphasized that such quotations are to be treated with the very greatest caution, for even the best writers when they are exercising the greatest care make serious mistakes. I wish to add two illustrations to those already given: When Macaulay wrote for the *Edinburgh Review* a review of Gleig's *Warren Hastings* he referred with great scorn to the literary inferiority of *The Vicar of Wakefield,* yet thought he had said *The History of Greece.* And he could never explain how he had written one thing when he believed he had written another. The most remarkable error of this sort with which I am familiar is Moore's quotation of Byron's *Don Juan,* IV, 4 as the words of Shakespeare, after he had already correctly quoted them in his own *Life of Byron.*[9]

The first poem to be clearly assigned to Homer by a reliable author, except the two great epics, is the *Hymn to Apollo,* which is quoted as Homeric by Thucydides (III, 104). *The Margites,* a lampoon or literary caricature, was regarded as Homeric by Aristotle, who was probably voicing an inherited tradition, although the evidence that Archilochus and Aristophanes regarded this poem as Homeric is extremely weak. The first poems to be attached to the author of the Iliad and the Odyssey were these little poems of unknown origin, then others were assigned to that great name until, in the intellectual darkness which followed, Homer was regarded as the source of all early poetry. A comparison of the poems listed as Homeric by Xenophon, Plato, and Aristotle with those so given by Suidas will show which

[9] *Table Talk of Samuel Rogers,* London, 1903, 223.

way the current was running, and will clearly
indicate whether poems were being taken from
or added to the name of Homer. We cannot
by taking the ignorant assertions of these late
writers and by setting aside the explicit statements of the ablest thinkers of Alexandria and
of Athens arrive at earlier truth. Suidas, Tzetzes,
and Aelian are not such safe witnesses for Hellas
of the fifth century as are Isocrates, Xenophon,
Plato, and Aristotle.

CHAPTER II

THE ARGUMENTS OF WOLF

With Aristotle the works of creative genius for the most part ceased, and the year of his death, 322 B.C., closed that long and brilliant era which is commonly known as Classical Greece. Not a trace of proof has ever been found that during the classical period anyone questioned the unity of the Iliad and the Odyssey or that they were both the work of one poet, and that poet, Homer. During the following years the Greeks lost their independence and by reason of their lack of political power and of the productive influence which that power called forth, they turned either to problems of scholarship or to the exercise of their great talents for subtle argumentation. One of these subtle exercises of the power to reason was the attempt to prove that the Iliad and the Odyssey were by different authors. They seem to have made no effort to find who these authors were, but to have been satisfied in producing arguments for diversity. Whether these arguments were meant seriously or were simply an attempt to apply to Homer that vaunted skill of proving either side of any question we do not know. But the greatest of the Alexandrian scholars, Aristarchus, wrote replies which he named *Answers to the paradox of Xenon,* as if he regarded the so-called chorizontic arguments as merely sophistic attempts to prove the improbable or the impossible.

These arguments seem to have been regarded solely as an exercise in argumentation and they were without any known effect on the study of Homer. Seneca *De Brev. Vitae* 13, refers to that vice clinging to the Greeks of questioning, "How many men did Ulysses have?" "Which was written earlier, the Iliad or the Odyssey?" "Did the same poet write both poems?" Lucian, the leading Greek writer of the second century of our era, imagines that he had been admitted into the sacred presence of Homer, whom he questioned in regard to the disputed facts of the poet's life and writings. Lucian learns from the poet himself his origin, and the reason for beginning his poem with the Wrath; learns that the verses rejected by the Alexandrians are genuine, and that the Iliad was written before the Odyssey, and from observation he saw that the poet had not been blind.[1] There is no reference in Lucian to any doubts cast on the authorship of the Iliad and the Odyssey. The author of the piece of literary criticism, *De Sublimitate,* formerly supposed to be Longinus, in an elaborate discussion of the characteristics of Homeric poetry gives no trace of any opinion which assigns the Iliad and the Odyssey to different authors.

[1] Lucian, *Vera Historia* II, 20.

The entire lack of any following and also the fact that the separatist arguments were called paradoxes by Aristarchus and referred to by Seneca as an example of that Greek perversity in seeking absurd themes for arguing, as well as the silences of Lucian and Longinus, convince me that the so-called chorizontic movement of the early Alexandrian period was simply a piece of argumentation, an exercise in dialectics, and had nothing in common with literary criticism. Except for this utterly vain and ineffectual paradoxical reasoning of Xenon and Hellanicus we hear of no arguments advanced by either Greek or Latin writers to show that Homer was not the creator of both the Iliad and the Odyssey.

Others may have anticipated him in many or in all of his theories, but the Homeric Question was definitely and scientifically launched by Friedrich August Wolf in his famous *Prolegomena, Volumen I,* published in 1795, the influence of which has permeated all fields of classical and Biblical literature. Two circumstances have contributed to the great importance of this work of Wolf: first, it came at a time when the French Revolution had filled the earth with general skepticism and with distrust in inherited beliefs and existing institutions. Everything went into the caldron of doubt. The leaders in this movement, with its glorification of the common man, the mass, felt called upon to challenge the claims of genius and to assert that what had been regarded as the work of the superman was, in fact, the production of the people, the fruit of whose achievements had been wrested from them. The Iliad and the Odyssey were but folk-poetry, the poetic expression of the entire people, and not the creation of any single superior genius. Marx, under the same spell, later argued that all wealth is produced by labor, by the common man, and that a few have taken to themselves or exploited the work of the many; so in a somewhat similar way it was assumed that epic poetry was the production of the entire people and that a real or hypothetical Homer had exploited the people of its poetry.

The second reason contributing to the enormous popularity of the Homeric Question lies in the fact that for about a century and a quarter certain types of universities and certain types of scholarship have dominated the learning of the world. In these universities promotions have generally been in exact ratio to the number of pages of articles, pamphlets, or books published. It has almost been an actionable offense to say of a professor, "He is an inspiring teacher," which would be like saying of a woman, "She has a good heart" or "She means well." The real praise is to say of him, "He is a productive scholar," a "productive scholar" being one who publishes a certain number of pages per year, pages which are always counted and are rarely weighed. The Homeric Question furnished inexhaustible mater-

ial for numberless pages; you did not need to read
what others had written, since you could always
create a new theory of your own. You did not
even need to read Homer. All you needed was
paper, ink, and audacity. Here anyone could be
a millionaire and required no capital to start in
business. The field was unlimited, you could
either discuss what Homer had said, or, if you
did not care to read Homer, you could write a
book on what he should have said. Wilamowitz,
the most radical of critics, practically throws
away all the present Iliad and reconstructs a new
Iliad, "an Iliad worthy of a great poet." The
immense popularity of the Homeric Question has
largely consisted in the fact that it put no re-
straint on imaginative or creative and productive
scholarship. It did not demand as a prerequisite
a knowledge of the thing discussed, for one could
always escape the charge of ignorance of Homer
by pointing out that the verses quoted against
him had been rejected by a whole set of critics.
As every verse in Homer has been pronounced
late by some high authority, the answer was
always ready and always complete. If the question of Homeric authorship were as settled as
that of Sophocles or Milton, then a real knowledge
of the subject must precede all articles or books
on Homer and the field would thus be immeasur-
ably reduced.

The main argument advanced by Wolf for
doubting the unity of the Iliad rested on the

assumption that writing was unknown at the time the Iliad originated, or so little known that it could not be used for literary purposes, and without writing Wolf regarded it as impossible that a poem of such bulk as the Iliad should either have been composed or preserved. He argued also that even if poems of the size of the Iliad and the Odyssey had been composed there would have been no occasion for their delivery, since no audience could have been found willing or capable of listening to poems of such magnitude. He assumed that the Iliad must have been composed of a mass of songs, more or less independent, songs undergoing constant alterations until they were collected into one poem under the orders of Peisistratus, who appointed a commission for that purpose. Homer by this process was eliminated and, whoever may have composed the different songs, the Iliad itself is a learned creation mechanically put together about the middle of the sixth century B.C. That great argument of Wolf in regard to writing, around which the Homeric Question so long revolved, has now been abandoned, so that it is hardly worth the effort to storm a position which has long been deserted and which no one today would care to defend.

The second argument was that, even if such poems had been composed, their bulk would be so great that they could not be recited, and also there could have been no occasion for their delivery. It was not necessary that either poem be repeated

entire at one time. It must be remembered that
many of our best literary productions appeared
in serial form in magazines having only monthly
or quarterly issues. It is quite as easy to suppose
that an audience could receive the Iliad in install-
ments as it could a *Sartor Resartus* or a *Vanity
Fair*. We must not forget, however, that there is
one great difference between an ancient and a
modern audience and that is the immense diversity of the claims on the modern reader in comparison with the ancient hearer. We know that
the Greeks would assemble from dawn to dark
for several consecutive days in order that they
might listen with rapture to the productions of
a dramatic festival. It is very doubtful if this
long literary festival of the drama was a complete
innovation. The conservative Greek may well
have followed, in listening to Aeschylus, Sophocles, and the other dramatic poets, the same habit
which had for ages made him familiar with
literary recitals covering several days. During
the last three days of the City Dionysia in Athens
nine tragedies, three satyric plays, and at least
three comedies were presented, or not less than
fifteen dramas, hence at least five on each day.
Some of the existing dramas contain over seventeen hundred verses, but the average is not far
from fourteen hundred. Each day, therefore,
would see about seven thousand verses presented
by actor or chorus. In all the plays the movements of the chorus, the pauses in action, and

the dramatic silences no doubt so prolonged
the time of delivery that these seven thousand
dramatic verses must have occupied as much time
as would be taken by ten thousand epic verses,
recited by single bards. It is therefore clear that
the last three days of the City Dionysia involved
quite as much strain on the hearer as did the
recital of the entire Iliad and Odyssey. But the
last three days of the City Dionysia followed
another day or days just as strenuous, since the
dramas came after the audience had already
listened to ten dithyrambic choruses.[2] Even Greek
tragedy had no such grasp on the Greek mind
and Greek enthusiasm as that held by Homer, so
that it is far easier to picture them listening to
the entire Iliad and Odyssey than to fifteen or
more dramas in three consecutive days. The
assumption, then, that there was no occasion on
which the Iliad and the Odyssey could have been
presented collapses under the consideration of the
undoubted facts of Greek dramatic production.

The final argument was that these poems took
on their epic form in Athens under the leadership
of Peisistratus, hence the theory that under this
despot not only were the detached poems of
Homer united into epic wholes, but changes were
made in the text to glorify Athens and Peisistratus himself. These will be discussed in reverse
order, first, the probability that interpolations
were made in the interest of Athens, and, second,

[2] Flickinger, *The Greek Theater and Its Drama,* 196 ff.

the part taken by Athens and Peisistratus in the creation or preservation of the Iliad and the Odyssey.

The first writer to refer to interpolations in the interest of Athens is Diogenes Laertius, a writer presumably of the second century of our era, who in his *Life of Solon,* chap. 48, says: "It is reported that Solon wrote in the Catalogue the verse which makes Ajax draw up his ships next to the Athenians." In chapter 57 this same Diogenes Laertius gives Dieuchidas, a writer of Megara, as the source for this statement. Tradition varies between Solon and Peisistratus as the forger of that verse, but the theory of Athenian interpolation is not supported by any good early literary or historical authority. It rests chiefly on the evidence furnished by the poems themselves. We have all the facts a Megarian or a Diogenes Laertius had and we can test for ourselves the probability of interpolations in the interest of Athens.

Attica and Athens must have existed long before Homer. Excavations show that in the vicinity of Athens was an important center of Mycenaean culture, so that any poem dealing in a large way with a general expedition undertaken by the Greeks of that age must assign a part, presumably a large part, to Athens.

How prominent in Homer are the warriors from this Mycenaean center? In the first book of the Iliad the poet introduces Achilles, Agamemnon, Ajax, Idomeneus, Menelaus, Nestor, Odysseus, and Patroclus; and Diomede appears early in the second book. It is not until the Catalogue of the Ships that a single Athenian is named, and then only in a sort of geographical survey, where the poet, having described the forces from Bœotia and the intervening or adjoining regions, passes to Athens and to Salamis, then on to Argos and to Tiryns. The bitterest enemy of Athens could hardly have omitted Attica in this general survey. Athens is there represented by a single leader, Menestheus, a leader in whom the Athenians took no pride, so little pride indeed that Euripides, when telling the story, despite Homer, substituted another leader, whose memory would arouse the interest and the enthusiasm of his own countrymen.[3]

This Menestheus next appears in Δ 338, when Agamemnon sternly rebukes him for his listless inactivity in a time of danger, while Menestheus in silence listens to the reproof. His next appearance is at M 331, when, terrified by the approach of the Lycian leaders, he sends for the help of Ajax, who comes and rescues him. It seems odd that the Athenians, who are assumed to have laid claim to the island of Salamis because of their relations with Ajax, should have either interpolated or preserved these verses in which their own timid champion was rescued by the leader of the very island over which they claimed control. Why

[3] *Iph. in Aulis*, 247.

did they not reverse it, and have Ajax rescued by Menestheus? They could then support their own claim by an epic obligation. In N 685 is pictured the failure of Menestheus and his men to keep Hector from the ships, and in O 329 Menestheus is utterly unable to save Stichius, an Athenian, from Hector, and Iasus, also an Athenian, from Aeneas. Menestheus is not mentioned again in Homer, not even reappearing at the final review of the Greeks to take part in the games held in honor of Patroclus. These three generals, Stichius, Iasus, and Menestheus, are the sole representatives of Athens named in Homer, the first two being introduced only to be slain, and having no voice nor part in the poem. Menestheus, the Athenian leader, is never consulted, is spoken to but once, and then in severest rebuke, speaks but a single time and that in a plea for help, sees his companions fall at his side, helpless to save them, does no act of valor, however slight, and passes from notice early in the course of the poem. If such a hero was created to exalt Athenian pride, then that pride was easily exalted and easily satisfied.

The verses selected as proof of forgery in the interest of Athens are B 557 f., "Ajax brought twelve ships from Salamis and bringing them moored them where the hosts of the Athenians stood." The second verse is referred to as if genuine by Aristotle (*Rhet.* i, 15), but Megarian sources claimed it was a forgery inserted to

decide or strengthen the claims of the Athenians
to the island of Salamis in their contest with
Megara. Zenodotus and Aristarchus appear to
have passed in silence the charge of Athenian
interpolation, even though they did not admit
this verse into their text.

Homer consistently keeps Ajax near the
Athenians; Menestheus and his men were rescued
by Ajax from the Lycians in M 339 ff. In the
fierce fight between Hector and Ajax (N 185 ff.),
Amphimachus is slain, and his body is rescued and
carried back to the line of the Achaeans by two
Athenians, Menestheus and Stichius. These same
Athenians (N 865 ff.) try in vain to restrain Hector in his attack on Ajax. In the great struggle
between Ajax and Hector (O 329 ff.), Stichius and
Iasus, the two Athenian companions of Menestheus, are slain. Once only is Menestheus apparently away from Ajax, and that is in the review
of the army made by the king in Δ, where Agamemnon upbraids him and Odysseus, but soon after
(Δ 489) Antiphus hurls at Ajax, misses him, and
hits a companion of Odysseus; now Menestheus
and Odysseus entered the fight as companions,
hence even here Ajax was fighting near the
Athenians, and Ajax, Odysseus, and Menestheus
must have stood close together.

This hidden proof of the intimate relations
existing between Ajax and the Athenians can not
be due to an interpolator, but must come from
the original poet. This subtle harmony is not

an addition, it is the hidden harmony of the
whole. The poet who wrote the suspected line
had the same idea whenever he referred to Ajax
and the Athenians.

This suspected verse is the only one in the
Iliad which gives a home to Ajax, and it seems
most unlikely that this mighty chieftain, second
only to Achilles, should be a warrior without a
home and without a country. It has long been
observed that most of the Homeric heroes moved
to and from the battle in a chariot, but sweating
Ajax, loaded with his ponderous shield, moved
always on foot and had neither a driver nor a
chariot. This trait he shared with Odysseus, who
came from the little island of Ithaca, and it is fair
evidence that he, too, came from some island
too small to train its inhabitants in the use of
the chariot. This small island is named in the
suspected verse and in none other in the Iliad.
Inasmuch as Ajax is homeless without this verse,
since the absence of a chariot marks him as an
islander, since he is regularly near the Athenians,
and since Aristotle refers without questioning to
this verse as Homeric, I regard it as genuine and
as a part of the original conception of the Iliad.

The references to Athens in the Odyssey are
few and vague, never joined to any praise of that
city: once Sunium is named as the promontory of
Athens; once Odysseus tells how he saw Ariadne
whom Artemis slew as she was going from Crete
to Athens; once it is said that Orestes returned

from Athens to slay the murderer of his father;
and once it is said that Athena came to Marathon
and Athens of wide streets. These are all the
direct references to Athens in the Odyssey. But
two of them are highly significant, for the simple
statement that "Orestes returned from Athens"
is at complete variance with Athenian tradition,
since it was one of the commonplaces of the Attic
traditions that Orestes came from Phocis. If
Athenian pride inserted Athens here in Homer,
why did that same pride retain Phocis in tragedy?
If Athens ever controlled Homeric tradition, why
was the word Athens not changed to Phocis?
The answer seems simple: The word was in Homer
in spite of Athenian traditions, and no one in
Athens had power to change it. The other significant passage is η 80, where it is said that
"Athena left Scheria and came to Marathon and
to Athens." This has been regarded as the sure
proof of tampering with the text of Homer, and
Seeck, who sees many defects on many pages of
Homer, says: "That the goddess should have come
from Phaeacia, that is from the west, and pass over
the east coast of Attica before coming to Athens is
highly unreasonable. If the poet in spite of this
names Marathon, it could only be from personal
grounds. In all probability Marathon was his
home."[4] The last sentence he puts in italics.
That is to say, the poem contains a serious
blunder in the matter of the geography of Athens,

[4] Seeck, *Quellen der Od.*, 335.

a blunder self-evident to any Athenian, hence the
passage must have been due to an inhabitant of
Attica, an inhabitant who knew better, so that
he might delight his own fellow-countrymen, who
also knew better.   This very inaccuracy shows
that the verses were composed by a poet with only
a vague idea of the relative positions of Athens
and Marathon, composed also for an audience
with the same indefinite ideas.   Homer had no
maps or charts before him and would be expected
to have this indefinite grasp of direction in regard
to lands somewhat remote.   This vagueness is of
a piece with the belief of Nestor that birds of
passage could not cross the Mediterranean in a
single year (γ 321) or the statement of Menelaus
that Pharos is a long day's sail from the mouth
of the Nile (δ 355).   Also, in general connection
with the influence of Athens on Homeric poetry,
the fact must not be forgotten that the word
Athens is found in but a single passage in the
Iliad and that in the general geographical survey
of the Catalogue.

It has been a common presumption of the
critics that the men who collected or created the
Iliad and the Odyssey for Peisistratus added to
the Odyssey a son of Nestor, whom they named
Peisistratus in order to flatter the tyrant.   This
youthful Peisistratus is one of the least important
actors of the poem.   He was created to accompany
Telemachus to Sparta, and when that is done he is
completely ignored.   After he and Telemachus

part company (o 215), he is forgotten, even his
companion does not bid him any farewells, for
he simply leaves him. The poet makes no mention of his reception by his father, and he does
not allow him to tell the story of the trip to
Sparta. The significant fact, however, is that
when Telemachus narrates to his mother the tale
of that journey he never mentions Peisistratus
nor refers to him in any way; clear proof that he
was a person in whom the poet and the hearer had
only a secondary interest. Such a character is
the creation of the original poet and has no marks
of the flatterer, for there is nothing in it to flatter
anyone, certainly not the tyrant of Athens.

The positive proofs that the Homeric poems
were never under Attic control are many. In
Homer Oedipus died in Thebes (Ψ 679), although
one of the greatest plays of Sophocles is founded
on the story of his death in Colonus, a suburb of
Athens; Tydeus was buried in Thebes (Ξ 114),
yet the Athenians prided themselves on his burial
at Eleusis; Philomela is the daughter of Pan-
dareus (τ 518), not of the Athenian Pandion;
Hecuba is the daughter of Dymas (Π 718), but
in Attic traditions she was the daughter of
Cisseus; Orestes returns to his home from Athens
(γ 307), not from Phocis; Agamemnon's daugh-
ters have names utterly unlike the names given
them by the Athenians (I 145). How easily an
Athenian could have substituted the Attic Iphigeneia for the Homeric Iphianassa! The hero

of the Odyssey reappears as the villain of Attic tragedy; the kindly, gentle host and friend, Menelaus, becomes almost inhuman; and Minos, the Cretan tyrant, who demanded the annual sacrifice of fourteen Athenian youths to the Minotaur, is, in Homer, the wise judge, the friend and companion of Zeus. It is beyond belief that the Athenians ever had such control of these poems as to insert Peisistratus into the story of the Odyssey and to reshape them at will, yet never took the pains to rewrite these traditions which could have been so easily changed. To see how an Athenian who really had a free hand dealt with Homeric traditions, we need only turn to Euripides, who, in his *Iphigeneia in Aulis,* substituted another leader for Homer's Menestheus and, in spite of the definite number of fifty ships named in the Catalogue, increased the Athenian contingent to sixty, while Argos is made inferior by reducing its ships from eighty to fifty. The internal evidence furnishes no proof that any changes were made in the text of Homer in the interest of Athens. Moreover, if Athens had absolute control of these poems, the failure to bring them into harmony with Athenian pride and Athenian traditions is one of the most inexplicable things in literature.

What external proofs are there that Athens or Peisistratus ever controlled this poetry? The story of Peisistratus and Homer seems to have originated in the hostile state of Megara, where political enmity sought to console itself by claim-

ing it had lost by fraud what it could not gain
by force. No admirer of Peisistratus has been
able to show that any intellectual life was called
into being by him or by his sons. It is true that
Onomacritus was detected in forging a prophecy
for these superstitious despots, and Herodotus
tells of their great interest in signs, omens, and
oracles, but neither he nor any early writer gives
the slightest indication that any creative intellectual or literary impulse came from that family.
The Peisistratidae might have had the wealth to
employ and the taste to appreciate the praises
or the songs of an Anacreon or a Simonides, but
the literary barrenness of Athens during their
lives and during the years immediately following
gives no indication that they furnished any stim-
ulus to literary activity. The story that Peisistratus founded a great library and was the patron
of letters seems pure fiction, for Aristotle in his
recently discovered *Athenian Constitution,* chap.
16, describes in great detail the work done by
Peisistratus, his criminal laws, and the fact that
he recognized therein extenuating circumstances,
his efforts to assist the poor farmers, and also
his democratic and philanthropic spirit, but he
makes no reference to his library or to his literary
pursuits. When we consider Aristotle's immense
enthusiasm for literature and for the gathering
of books, we are certain that he would never
have passed over in silence the great intellectual
achievements which the advocates of Peisistratus

as the creator of Homer so confidently assume. No writer, whose works have survived, connects Peisistratus with Homer until Cicero, and Cicero lived almost five hundred years after the time of Peisistratus. No later writer adds any detail which proves a new source of knowledge, hence the multiplication of the names of later writers referring to Peisistratus adds no strength to the argument.

There is not to be found in Herodotus, Plato, Aristotle, nor in any early Athenian writer a reference connecting the tyrant with Homer, nor is there a single allusion in all the great mass of learning referred to the scholars of Alexandria. Wolf's statement that the united voice of all antiquity consistently assigned to Peisistratus the honor of collecting, arranging, and putting into writing the poetry of Homer looks dangerously near intentional deception. Even more to the point is the fact that Herodotus says the Athenians used that passage in the Catalogue, which is now most suspected, to explain their unwillingness to yield the command of the fleet, at the time of the invasion of Xerxes, to any but Sparta, and he makes no comment. No one familiar with the method of Herodotus could suppose that he knew the Athenians were using a forged passage and yet concealed that knowledge. Again, when he described Onomacritus as one who had been exiled for interpolating a verse into the poetry of Musaeus, there can be no reasonable doubt that

he would have added that formerly this Onomacritus had been intrusted by Peisistratus with the
task of collecting the poetry of Homer and he had
also added verses thereto. It is incredible that
a public sentiment which exiled a man for interpolating a verse in so insignificant a poem as that
of Musaeus should have been indifferent to wholesale additions to the almost sacred poetry of
Homer.

In regard to the Megarian charge that the
Spartan arbitrators were tricked in awarding
Salamis to Athens because of an interpolated
verse, one of two things is true: either the poetry
of Homer was well-known at that time or it was
not. If well-known, an interpolation would have
been immediately detected; and if it was not well-
known, it would not have been accepted as the
ultimate authority. In all the attacks made later
on Athenian duplicity, no Spartan ever complains
of this deception, and no Athenian is ever quoted
as defending a proposed injustice by referring
to this clever imposture of the fathers.

There is no evidence for this Homeric recension under the supervision of Peisistratus but the
evidence of probabilities. What are the probabilities that in the second half of the sixth century
Homer came so completely under the control of
Athens that in a few years Athenian legates at
Syracuse could quote Athenian interpolations as
genuine and neither the speakers betray nor the
hearers suspect that the quoted verses were

spurious? In order to compel this complete and
rapid acceptance the Athenians must have had a
unique and commanding position both in government and in literature, so that all Hellas would
without questioning regard them as leaders. But
just the opposite is true, for in the years immediately following the fall of the family of Peisistratus, Athens was unable to settle her own domestic
affairs without the help or intervention of Sparta,
and in 480, ten years after Marathon, Athens
accepted her own inferiority as an established
fact and yielded to Sparta the right to command
both the naval and land forces in the struggle with
Xerxes. Weak as Athens was in a military and
political sense in the years before the Persian
Wars, her literary fame was even more feeble.
It is hard for us, with the glory of the fifth and
fourth centuries in our minds, to grasp how far
Athens lay outside the currents of literature until
the rise of the drama. The Muses were connected
with Helicon, Olympia, and Pieria, but there was
no mount of the Muses in Attica. Such early
fabled bards as Linus, Thamyris, and Musaeus
were from other parts of Greece. No poem of the
Epic Cycle was ever assigned to an Attic poet and
we are told that Hesiod of Bœotia, Peisander of
Rhodes, Panyasis of Samos or of Halicarnassus,
and Antimachus of Colophon were regarded as the
greatest epic poets after Homer. No Athenian in
that list! Peisistratus lived in the age of the lyric
poets, yet not one of all the illustrious nine lyric

poets was born in Athens. What district adjacent to the Aegean Sea was so destitute of literary fame as Attica in 500 B.C.? If poetry was to be recited at the great festivals, the Athenians were obliged to adopt the works of a foreign poet, who sang the praises of rival nations, and if a living poet was desired, it was necessary to send abroad for an Anacreon or a Simonides. It could not have been either the political or literary position of Athens which compelled an early acceptance of an Attic version of Homer. Schools of Homeric enthusiasts flourished before the time of Peisistratus in many cities of Ionia and in the islands of the Aegean, from which a knowledge of Homer radiated to all parts of the Greek world. We have a long list of the names of those who busied themselves with investigations in regard to Homer and Homeric poetry, but not one of these early investigators was from Athens. Homeric poetry must have been known throughout Greece at the beginning of the sixth century, since it seems to be assumed as the setting or background for most of the earliest poetry. The exact condition of that age has been pictured by Xenophanes of Colophon, an early and a competent authority, born at about the time of the usurpation of Peisistratus, and therefore trained in Ionia in the version then current, before any recension by the tyrant was possible. He regarded the familiarity with Homer as universal, something all had known from earliest childhood. This Xenophanes was much offended by the immorality of the Homeric gods and severely criticised the poet for his descriptions of divine baseness. To him Hiero, the tyrant of Syracuse, is assumed to have replied, "This Homer whom you revile, although dead, continues to support ten thousand servants, while you with difficulty can maintain but two." Even if this story be apocryphal, it gives some indication of the great popularity of Homeric poetry. We know that the recitation of Homeric poetry was early established as a custom in Sicyon, for Cleisthenes in jealousy of Argos forbade the Homeric bards the privilege of public recital. This expulsion of these bards must have been at least a generation before Peisistratus could have revised the poems.

The entire Greek world at that time regarded Homer as its teacher and its prophet. Was that world likely to exchange the Homer it knew for a strange and interpolated Homer? The Greeks were always a conservative people, extremely tenacious of old customs and of old institutions, so that epic poetry continued to be composed for more than a thousand years in the verse and dialect of Homer; Tyrtaeus, the great Lacedaemonian war poet, might compose his fiery anapaests in the native dialect of Sparta, but when he used dactyls, he must show their Ionic origin; and even an Athenian dramatist, when composing for an Athenian audience, felt it necessary to give a foreign color to his choral songs, since they must

show their alien birth. This persistent conservatism of the Athenians, despite the ruin brought
by Persian fire and devastation, repeatedly ham-
pered Pericles in his plans for beautifying the
Acropolis, and this conservatism gave to the
Amphictyonic Council that power which was made
in the hands of Philip so disastrous to the liberty
of Greece.[5]

This conservatism is the very breath of Greece
and still survives. In November, 1901, the public
use of a revised text of the Bible led to a bloody
riot in which eight persons were slain, the min-
istry overthrown, and the Metropolitan forced
to flee; and in 1903 an attempt to produce in
the theater a play of Aeschylus in modernized
speech led to a riot. In view of this Hellenic
trait it seems incredible that Homeric bards and
scholars should abandon the Homer they knew
and without a murmur accept the interpolated
edition of a state so obscure intellectually and
politically as Athens was at the end of the sixth
century. This Peisistratean theory involves not
only their acceptance of this Athenian Homer, but
their silent acceptance as well, since no writer has
ever mentioned any struggle as arising from the
change.

It must be remembered that there never was
in historical times anything resembling a united
Greece. Even in the Persian Wars many of the

---

[5] A fuller discussion of Athenian influence on the text of
Homer, with reference to the recent literature, has been published
in *Class. Phil.* VI, 419 ff. and IX, 395 ff.

Greek states joined the foe, and in such patriotic states as Athens there seems to have been a pro-Persian party. There never was a united Greece and there never was any body of men who formed a literary Academy or Sanhedrin, competent and authorized to pass on questions of poetry and revisions of text; so that even if Peisistratus had revised Homer there was no power in Greece to bring about its unquestioned acceptance. The most improbable thing in regard to this theory is that Greek bards would all have accepted a new version in absolute silence and no one would have raised his voice in protest.

Attention has already been called to the fact that Onomacritus was banished in the time of Peisistratus for adding a verse to the poetry of Musaeus, and in a later age Lycon, the comic actor and friend of Alexander, was fined the enormous sum of ten talents for interpolating a single line in a comedy, a fine which would have ruined him had it not been paid by Alexander.[6] A public sentiment which would not tolerate these trifling changes in minor authors never grew up among a people accustomed to wholesale changes in the almost sacred text of Homer.

The great scholars of Alexandria never referred to the work of Peisistratus, and although they quote manuscripts of Homer which came from Sinope, Crete, Cyprus, Chios, Marseilles, and the most diverse parts of Greece, they never

6 Flickinger, *op. cit.*, 191.

mention a manuscript as coming from Athens. Equally significant is the fact that no one of the great Homeric scholars was a native of Attica.

The knowledge of Homer in an age before a reading public was possible must for the most part have been carried from place to place by reciters or rhapsodes. Therefore, if an Athenian version of the sixth century was to take the place of an earlier version, it must have been carried to favor by rhapsodes from Athens. Yet we have no knowledge of any such Athenian reciters. The classical description of these wandering Homeric evangelists is given by Plato in his *Ion*. From this we learn that even in Athens that famous reciter was from Ephesus, and those especially renowned for their appreciation and interpretation of Homer were Metrodorus of Lampsacus, Stesimbrotus of Thasos, and Glaucon, apparently from Rhegium; yet if Homer were really "The Gift of Athens," as Professor Gilbert Murray asserts, it seems too much to believe that Ionian bards would come to Athens, exchange their Homer for a new version, but never make a reference to that fact. In Athens nearly all forms of Greek art and literature reached their perfection. The Ionic and Doric columns originated elsewhere, but the best of each has been found at Athens; philosophy had its birth in Ionia, but the greatest philosophers were Socrates, Plato, and Aristotle; histories also were first written

on the eastern shores of the Aegean, but the
greatest history was the work of Thucydides.
Rhetoric, oratory, comedy, and tragedy originated
outside of Attica, but all reached their zenith
there. The epic alone of all the early forms of
literature seems never to have stirred the creative
genius of Attica—no Athenian has ever been mentioned who gained distinction by the creation of
epic poetry. It is evident that Athens lay outside
those movements which created and preserved the
epic treatment of heroic tales.

How did the tradition in regard to Peisistratus
arise? Athens in common with other Greek states
had public recitations of Homeric poetry, and
somehow a regulation came into force forbidding
the reciter to cull out the portions which would
win the greatest favor, and commanding him to
follow the established order of the poems; that
is, a bard could not recite the "Parting of Hector
and Andromache," then follow it with the "Death
of Hector," since all the advantage would be with
the bard who recited first. The first bard must
recite the poem in its accepted order, and the
second bard must take up the story where the
first had left off. The very fact that such decrees
could be deemed necessary shows that there was
even then an established sequence, for discon-
nected songs could have no regular order. The
scholiast to Pindar (*N.* ii, 2) says: "The poetry
of Homer being delivered in portions formerly,

each of the contestants recited whatever part he wished.'' Thus this simple regulation was intended to give each contestant a fair chance by prohibiting the early contenders from selecting all the choicest portions. This is the ''scattered songs of Homer,'' which has given rise to the myth of Peisistratus as the preserver of the Homeric songs and the creator of the Homeric epics. The theory that the Homer recited at the Great Panathenaic Festival included all the great mass of early poetry, is utterly discredited by the words of the orator Lycurgus (chap. 26) : ''Our fathers forbade the recitation of any other poetry than that of Homer'' and by the clear statement of Isocrates that Homer's greatness in the eyes of the fathers consisted in the fact that he pictured the Greeks not as fighting each other but the barbarians (*Panegyricus* 159).

The theory that men who never wrote a great line of poetry could with scissors and paste create the two greatest poems of the world shows the fathomless depths of human credulity. Bentley, England's foremost scholar and most famous critic, has in his edition of Milton given for all time the classic example of the huge chasm between pure erudition and high poetry. Two quotations from this edition of Bentley will illustrate.

> No light, but rather darkness visible
> Served only to discover sights of woe.
> —Milton *P. L.* I, 63 f.

To the learned and reasoning brain of Bentley
"darkness visible" was a monstrosity, so he made
sense by changing it thus:

> No light, but rather a transpicuous gloom.

And

> Our torments also may, in length of time,
> Become our elements.
>> —*P. L.* II, 274.

This becomes under the learned touch of Bentley:

> Thus, as was well-observed, our torments may
> Become our elements.

It seems incredible that any one could have suggested the prose phrase "as was well-observed"
as an improvement of Milton.

The constant assumption made by all the
critics that meaningless or contradictory scenes
were added to the poems has never presented any
satisfactory grounds for explaining why a people
of the acute literary sense of the Greeks would
accept these postulated blunders. Two things are
necessary for such interpolations: first, stupid
bards, and, second, stupid audiences. Theognis
in the beginning of his poem says: "No one will
accept the worse, when the better is present."
But this interpolation theory just reverses that
and proclaims: "No one will keep the better,
when the worse is present"—not only keep the
worse, but cast out and forget the better. I wish
Wilamowitz or some other prophet of the gospel
of the better Iliad destroyed to make room for

the inferior would illustrate by concrete examples where the Greeks destroyed the good to make way for the bad. They might remove the inferior to put in its place the better or the perfect, but where have they admitted the bad when the good was at hand? An artistic sense which demanded the literary finish of the Pindaric odes, which called into being the dramas of Sophocles, and made Demosthenes strive for the very perfection of oratorical expression, was the public sentiment which the critics assume quietly accepted interpolations that defaced the most cherished of all their possessions, the poetry of Homer.

Not only were no changes made in the text of Homer by Peisistratus, but no one before him or after him has succeeded in materially altering the Homeric text. No two persons could copy the same words in exactly the same way, lines from memory would slip in, others would drop out, but no passage so extended as ten verses has been lost from or added to the poetry of Homer. Also the language of the present Vulgate is essentially the same as that in which the poems were originally composed. All quotations made from Homer are in virtually the same dialect as that found in the existing manuscripts, and, whatever the native speech of the writer, the language of Homer was not changed into that speech; Herodotus of Halicarnassus, Plato of Athens, Timaeus of Sicily, Plutarch of Bœotia, and Strabo of Pontus, all quote Homer in the same dialect, with no attempt to change his speech into their own vernacular. These men could paraphrase Homer, each in his own speech, but when quoting him as poetry, the language or dialect of the poem remained Homeric.

There is one proof that there never was any serious or conscious attempt to modernize the poetry of Homer which more than answers all contrary arguments, and that is the evidence of the lost letter, the consonant digamma. We know since the time of Bentley that the poetry of Homer in all parts of the poems made use of a letter which was early lost in Ionic Greek[7] and which never appeared in Attic literature, and in general was unsuspected by the bards or scholars to whom we owe the preservation of the poems of Homer. The loss of this letter caused apparent anarchy in the Homeric meter and seemingly permitted a word ending in a short vowel to be followed by an initial vowel, the forbidden hiatus, or permitted a short vowel to be scanned as long before a single consonant. The restoration to Homer of this lost consonant is regarded as one of the greatest feats of modern scholarship.

These apparent metrical defects were the despair of Homeric editors and greatly discounted the fame of the poet until Bentley proved that nearly all these defects could be righted on the theory that this consonant, which survived longer

[7] Smyth, *Greek Dialects,* 389: ''The sound of digamma was practically dead in Asia Minor at least by the year 700 B.C. and in Attika by the commencement of the sixth century.''

in other dialects, had been lost out of the poems
since their creation. It was very easy to insert
the digamma in most cases, and no scholar now
doubts that this letter belonged to the early
Homeric alphabet, whether that letter was written, or simply understood from the familiarity of
the hearers with its sound.

It would have been easy indeed for the preservers of Homer to have obliterated all traces
of this metrical difficulty by the slightest bits of
emendation, some so easy that we can hardly
understand why they preserved this hiatus when
the application of the rudimentary principles of
the Greek language would have removed it. A
simple rule of Ionic-Attic Greek is that the negative οὐ becomes οὐκ or οὐχ before an initial vowel,
yet we have οὔ ἕθεν (A 114. Ludwich in a critical
note to this reading adds the significant words
"οὐχ meorum nullus."), οὔ οἱ, B 392, E 53, Ξ 141,
O 496, P 153, T 124, Υ 349, X 219, α 262, θ 175, ν 417,
σ 355. Another simple rule concerns words ending
in epsilon and a nu-movable before a word beginning with a vowel, something akin to the English
use of the indefinite article a or an; but Homer has
κέ οἱ (Z 281, I 157), and often κέ ἑ (I 155). It is
remarkable that such an ill-sounding combination
should be preserved in any manuscript. δαῖέ οἱ
(E 4) is preserved in practically all manuscripts,
and even the difficult combination οὔ ἑ (Ω 214) is
preserved in many manuscripts. In all these
examples corrections made on the simplest prin-

ciples of Greek euphony would have removed every difficulty and would have obliterated all traces of the digamma.

The fact that these changes were not made shows that the language of Homer was a thing apart. They might paraphrase the poem into their own speech; they might even add an alternate verse to each verse of the original; they might parody it at will; yet the text itself was sacred and kept unchanged. A certain amount of change would seem inevitable, but Athenaeus, about 200 A.D., Eustathius, about 1200 A.D., quote Homer in the same dialect in which he was quoted by Herodotus, Plato, and Aristotle, showing that during this interval of sixteen hundred years no changes of any moment had taken place in the text of Homer. And the fact that manuscripts have preserved the unmetrical οὕ ἕθεν, οὕ οἱ, δαίέ οἱ, κέ ἑ, after the knowledge of digamma had vanished and when easy corrections were almost obligatory, carries its own proof that those who would not make these simple alterations never subjected Homer to the violent changes assumed by all the radical school.

Had the Homeric scholars of more than two thousand years ago been as reckless with the inherited text of Homer as many modern editors, they would have so completely obliterated all traces of digamma that not even a Bentley could have suspected its existence. The undoubted fact that the Greeks who edited or preserved the text of Homer kept alive the proofs of a lost letter, a letter they did not comprehend, and preferred to hand on a text which seemed full of metrical errors rather than to apply simple and uniform laws of phonetics of their own language, convinces me that they have made no changes of a more difficult and intricate character, and that those who have so faithfully preserved for posterity this old and unused digamma can be trusted to have honestly conserved the text of Homer in those places where change would have been difficult to make and easy to detect. Men who will not swallow gnats may safely be trusted with camels.[8]

[8] I wish to acknowledge my great indebtedness to Professors Ludwich and Allen for much of the material used above. This indebtedness is specified in my two articles on ''Athenian Interpolations in Homer'' (*Class. Phil.*, VI, 419, and IX, 395).

CHAPTER III

THE LINGUISTIC ARGUMENTS

The forces set in motion by the arguments of Wolf had immediate and far-reaching influence, but it is highly significant that few German or English writers who have an independent literary reputation, apart from scholarship, have been permanently convinced that the poetry of Homer could have been created except by a single person. Goethe, who began to write about the poetry of Homer as early as 1766, or nearly thirty years before the work by Wolf appeared, was swept off his feet by the seeming authority and broad learning there displayed. He accepted what was declared to be the united historical testimony of antiquity and, although he was slow to give up his belief in a single Homer, expressed himself as relieved of the danger of challenging comparison in his own works with the great Homer, for now he could hope to rival one of the group who wrote the Iliad and the Odyssey, even if he could not the undivided Homer. In his *Hermann und Dorothea,* 294 ff., he rejoices that now he is not called upon to contend with gods, since there is no longer a single Homer. However, as he became more and more steeped in the poetry of Homer, he became once more convinced of Homeric unity, in spite of the historical proofs advanced by Wolf, and at that time unanswered; and he referred to Wolf as a beast of prey, *Raubgetier,* who had wounded and despoiled him. In 1827 he wrote his final opinion on Homer as follows: "Homer is a noble unity and the poems handed down under his name could have sprung only from one mighty genius."[1]

Schiller reread his Homer at the appearance of the *Prolegomena* and wrote to Goethe that he had actually been swimming in a sea of poetry; and later he referred to Wolf's theory as barbaric. Wieland still adhered to a single Homer, and Voss, ignorant of the weakness of the historical arguments so boldly advanced, wrote to Wolf: "In spite of all I still believe in one Iliad, in one Odyssey, and in one Homer as the sole father of them both." In the face of what seemed unanswerable proofs drawn from language, history, and archaeology, such eminent critics as De Quincey, Shelley, Matthew Arnold, and Andrew Lang have stoutly upheld, on poetic grounds alone, the unity of the Homeric poems. The fact that these men of letters felt the poetic necessity for unity, even though all other arguments seemed adverse, is a matter of the very greatest importance. In the long run it will be seen that, when the matter at issue is purely one of poetry, no man

[1] All references to Goethe are based on W. J. Keller, "Goethe's Estimate of the Greek and Latin Writers," University of Wisconsin *Bulletin,* No. 786.

in Germany was so competent a judge as Germany's greatest poet; and I am not likely to be worried by defects the grammarians discover when Goethe and Schiller could not find them.

Wolf's *Prolegomena* was called by him Volume One. In it he presented the external, the historical proofs, and reserved for Volume Two the internal proofs of diverse authorship. Voss wrote to him and urged him to hasten the second volume, using these words:

Grant that Homer could not write his own name, and so much will I concede that your arguments have almost demonstrated, still to my thinking that only enhances the glory of the poet. The unity of the poet, and the unity of his works, are to me unshaken ideas. But what then? I am no bigot in my creed, so as to close my ears against all arguments, and these arguments, let me say plainly, you now owe to us all, arguments drawn from the internal structure of the Homeric poems. You have wounded us, Mr. Wolf, in our affections, you have affronted us, Mr. Wolf, in our tenderest sensibilities. But still we are just men, ready to listen, willing to hear and forbear. Meanwhile the matter cannot rest here. You owe it, Mr. Wolf, to the dignity of the subject, not to keep back those proofs which doubtless you possess, proofs, observe, conclusive proofs.

Although Wolf lived twenty-nine years of active life after the appearance of Volume One, Volume Two never appeared, and nothing resembling it was found among his unpublished papers.

Wolf never attempted to furnish those internal proofs of diverse authorship. That task has been the chief occupation of most of his followers, and in their own minds they have brought forth such overwhelming evidence of contradictions and absurdities, such diversities of language, meter, customs, and civilization that the Homeric Question has been completely reversed. The doubt whether one genius could have created such wealth of poetry has become the assurance that no one man could be responsible for so many absurdities. It is no longer the envy of a Goethe which begrudges the awarding of so much glory to a single Homer, but the magnanimity of a Wilamowitz which acquits him of the crime. Fick, with righteous indignation, exclaims: "The present Odyssey is a crime against human intelligence."[2] Muelder with a touch of sadness remarks: "It is really too bad that the poet of the Odyssey tried his powers in a species of poetry for which he had neither the creative ability nor the powers of expression."[3] And Wilamowitz, convinced that no great poem could be produced by a group of men, devotes his energies to attempting to prove that Homer is but wretched poetry, and he scorns the "fanatics, defenders of unity, who admire the divine Homer."[4] The Iliad is a "miserable piece of patchwork," *ein übles Flickwerk*.[5] He regrets that most of the really

[2] *Die Entstehung der Odyssee*, 168.

[3] *Hermes* 28, 448. "Es ist eigentlich schade dass er seine Gestaltungskraft in den Dienst einer Dichtart gestellt hat, deren stoffliche Voraussetzungen und deren Ausdrucksmittel er auch nicht annähernd beherrschte."

[4] *Die Ilias und Homer*.

[5] *Idem*, 322.

great scenes of Homer, scenes he could so easily supply, have yielded to miserable and impossible pieces of poetic absurdity.

If Fick, Muelder, Wilamowitz, and the rest have won, they have banished Homer, and with him all the literature of Greece and Rome as well. For all their great writers regarded Homer as the perfection of literature, they set him up as the unapproachable, and if they failed so utterly in their calmest judgment, we can have but little interest in their own productions. We have the best possible evidence of their own literary wisdom in the works they themselves produced. When the age that could inspire and create a Plato and an Aristotle still regarded Homer as the perfection of literary achievement, I respect the opinion of that age. When Plato and Aristotle agree in regard to the supreme excellence of a Greek writer, I shall not question their judgment. If Milton, Tennyson, Matthew Arnold, and Lowell have ever called anything in English poetry perfect, I shall not be worried if some prosaic and foreign grammarian challenges that verdict.

If Homer is forced into poetic bankruptcy, then all Greece goes down in the wreck, for Plato, with the best of all that Greece had produced before him, called him "the wisest," "the best and most divine of poets," "the poet wise in all things," "the most poetic and the first of the writers of tragedy," and Aristotle said of him, "Homer the divine poet superior in all things to all others.'' If one declares a note worthless, that worthlessness includes not only the signers but the endorsers as well, and Homer is too heavily endorsed to be the only one involved in that failure, for he has the unlimited guaranty not only of the greatest writers of Greece, but of Cicero, Horace, Vergil, Seneca, and Quintilian, the greatest of Italy; and also of Goethe and Schiller, the greatest of Germany. It is hard to believe that the united opinion of the real literary leaders of civilization is so utterly mistaken. Not a single writer of early Greece ever detected one fault in Homer as poetry. All the criticism leveled by early philosophers at his poetry was aimed at the representation of the gods. Even Plato, who dreaded the moral results of a conception of the gods which made them treacherous, revengeful, deceitful, and immoral, still regarded Homer as ''the most divine of poets.''

It seems strange in the face of this unanimous opinion of the really great poets and writers of all ages that the disintegrating arguments of Wolf and his successors should have won so complete a victory that at the beginning of this century they were practically alone in the field. I heard Professor Seymour say in the summer of 1897, in a lecture delivered at the University of Chicago, that he knew of no competent scholar who believed in the unity of Homer. Harper's *Classical Dictionary,* published in 1896, says under the word ''Homer'': ''Probably no one who has a right to an opinion on the subject now holds to the unity of the poems." In Wright's *History of Greek Literature,* published in 1907, we read on page 31: "Time has repressed the Unitarians and all scholars are now Separatists." A little earlier Huxley enumerated in the list of the achievements of science the fact that the unity of authorship of the Iliad was successfully assailed by scientific criticism.[6] Lachmann, with that air of authority which most of the higher critics assume, wrote: "Any one who does not comprehend how Homer sprang from and through small songs will waste his time in studying either what I write or epic poetry itself, for he has not the ability to understand any part of either.'" Though the critics of Homer agreed that they had driven the one poet from the Iliad and the Odyssey, they agreed in nothing else, and if there was something like peace where once there had been controversy, it was not the peace which comes from harmony but from the conviction that nothing was left deserving a struggle.

In the last few years five of the champions of Homeric criticism, Fick, Robert, Muelder, Bethe, and Wilamowitz have set forth in detail what each regarded as the real and original Iliad. Fick thought that the part of the Iliad which was really worth while covered 1936 verses, or a trifle less than one-eighth of the poem. In this better and nobler Iliad there is no parting scene be-

6 Shorey, *Americana,* sub v. Homer.
7 Quoted by Gerlach, *Philologus,* XXX, 43.

tween Hector and Andromache, none of the great
speeches spoken by the ambassadors and Achilles
in Achilles' tent, no games, and nothing of that
most dramatic scene ever written, the scene between Achilles and Priam, when Priam obtained
the dead body of his son. Robert reconstructed
his better Iliad out of 2146 verses, excluding the
famous scene on the walls of Troy where Helen
pointed out to the aged Trojans the leaders of
the Greeks, and oddly enough he excludes the
account of the death of Hector, admitting but
four verses from that wonderful book. Bethe
puts the true Iliad at about 1300 verses, or practically one-twelfth of the entire poem. Wilamowitz casts out large portions of the Iliad, but
he regards Γ and Φ, books absolutely rejected by
Fick, Robert, and Bethe, as essentially original
and unchanged. Wilamowitz cannot reconstruct
an original poem out of the existing Iliad, since
he regards the present poem as for the most part
the work of blunderers and blockheads, men who
removed the old and the noble poetry and then
substituted inferior verses of their own or of
others for the great poetry of the original. These
better parts were all lost as soon as they were
removed, no one has ever quoted or referred to
them, and this greatest of all losses was never
suspected until discovered by the great critic in
our own day. Wilamowitz has been able to give
an outline of much of the better and nobler Iliad,
but has modestly refrained from writing in full

that greater poem which he regards as alone
worthy the world's mightiest poet. It is well
to observe, however, that Homer has long been
regarded as the greatest of all poets not because
of the poem which Wilamowitz imagines, but
because of the Iliad and the Odyssey which we
actually have. Homer's reputation depends on
no hypothetical creation but on poetry now existing. It was because of this poetry that a man of
Macaulay's vision and judgment reached the conclusion that Shakespeare alone could challenge
comparison with Homer.[8]

Muelder disagrees with all the rest and has
recreated an original Iliad of his own. He regards the parts commonly considered as late as
being early and the so-called early parts as late.
If the critics have agreed in anything they have
agreed in making the story of Achilles the oldest
parts of the poem, and they have regarded the
exploits of other Greek heroes as the work of
late bards, but Muelder thinks the story of
Achilles the latest of all, a sort of literary mortar
by which the older parts are held together.

These five men do not agree in regard to one
single verse, and every line in Homer has been
rejected by at least two of them. There can be
no Homeric scholarship, no literary appreciation,
under such leadership, for Homer ceases to be a
poet and his work poetry, and becomes merely a
theory of Fick, of Robert, of Muelder, of Bethe,

[8] Trevelyan, *Life and Letters of Macaulay*, Harpers, 1876,
II, 93.

of Wilamowitz, and of the rest. It has detached
itself from learning as well as from poetry, and
has simply become a game of blindman's buff in
a swamp, in which no one is able to catch anything, and the player has no idea of what he is
trying to catch. Homer in such hands will inspire
no more poetry. During more than a century
Homeric scholarship has devoted itself to the task
of finding errors, contradictions, and absurdities
in both poems, so that Wilamowitz, the last and
the mightiest of the revilers of the Iliad, in his
recent work has used practically every word and
form of contempt of which the German language
is capable. I notice the following words of appreciation of the genius of Homer in the few pages,
160–170, of his *Die Ilias und Homer: erbärmliche,
unerträglich, wie sehr sie gefallen hat, Das hat
der Bearbeiter nicht thun mögen, herzlich albern
und ganz zwecklos, unbehaglich, Der Dichter hat
recht flüchtig gearbeitet.* Yet Horace said of this
very poet, *qui nil molitur inepte.* Too bad that
Horace could not have taken a course on literary
appreciation under this great critic!

When I began my work as a student of Homer
it was in complete accord with the milder of these
disintegrating theories, and I had accepted for
my own belief the theory of Jebb, Leaf, and
Christ, known as the *Ur-Ilias,* or the Original-
Iliad theory, which presupposes an older poem in
which one hero was brought forward, an original
Iliad of moderate compass, containing the exploits

of Achilles as far as the slaying of Hector. To
this had been added by later hands most of the
scenes in which Achilles is not a participant, as
well as the scene with the ambassadors in I, the
games in Ψ, and the ransoming of the body of
Hector in Ω.

The books composing the story of Achilles
were supposed to have certain well-defined usages
of language, theology, and antiquities which separated them from the other books of the Iliad,
and these other books of the Iliad, though differing from the Achilleis, shared these differences
with the Odyssey. If there was any orthodox
Homeric opinion twenty years ago, it was that
the books of the Achilleis were clearly older than
the rest of the Iliad, and that the non-Achilleid
books of the Iliad furnished many evidences of
close affinity with the Odyssey. These arguments
were supported by most of the great names of
classical scholarship and, so far as I know, were
not seriously challenged. Such a man of letters
as Andrew Lang doubted the conclusions drawn
from these proofs, but the proofs themselves he
did not question.

The argument most used to prove that certain
books of the Iliad have peculiar and intimate
connection with the Odyssey is the argument
from vocabulary. The book to which this test
was most confidently applied was the tenth book
of the Iliad, the Doloneia. It was shown that this
tenth book has many words, the number being

seventeen, which are found in no other book of the Iliad; but, although found in no other book of the Iliad, they are found in the Odyssey. This has been the strong argument for the assertion that this tenth book of the Iliad is Odyssean and it has been repeated in practically all the adverse criticisms of this book.

Some years ago I thought this argument might be strengthened by extending a like investigation to all the books of the Iliad, for thus the strength of the connection between K and the Odyssey might be made more evident by contrast with the small number of Odyssean words found in other books of the Iliad. By Odyssean words is meant words used in the Odyssey and in but one book of the Iliad. To my surprise I found that A, one of the supposedly old books, had twenty-six words found only in that book of the Iliad and in the Odyssey; Λ, another presumably old book, had thirty-three such words; Π had also thirty-three Odyssean words; and X, the very heart of the Achilleis, actually had thirty-four. That is, each book of the "original Iliad" had about twice as many Odyssean words as K, yet for its Odyssean words this book had been exiled from the Iliad. It was found that no less than seventeen books of the Iliad had more Odyssean words than the Doloneia, so that a thorough application of the arguments of the critics makes this late book one of the oldest of the Iliad. The list of these words was published in *Classical Philology*, vol. V, so that anyone might test them for himself, but thus far no critic has tried to revive or to defend that argument for assigning the Doloneia to the poet of the Odyssey, as distinct from the poet of the Iliad. Each book of the Odyssey has certain words found only in that book and in the Iliad, each book of the Iliad has certain words found only in that book and in the Odyssey. Each book of the Iliad has its own peculiar relations with the Odyssey, each book of the Odyssey its own peculiar relations with the Iliad, so that the argument which assigns the Doloneia to the poet of the Odyssey assigns each book of the Iliad to that poet and in turn each book of the Odyssey to the poet of the Iliad.

When the article containing this list was written I was so cowed by the authority and the assurance of the critics, especially by such sentences as "No one who has a right to an opinion believes in the unity of Homer," that I referred to "the poets of the Iliad," not daring to believe the thing I felt was true, that there was only one poet after all. The arguments were too many and too strong against it.

Another most convincing test was the test offered by the use of abstract nouns, since it is evident that the adjective good must precede the abstract goodness, and holiness must presuppose an earlier word, holy. When I restudied the arguments drawn from the use of abstracts they seemed to me so conclusive that I was glad that

I had not in the article mentioned declared my belief in a single Homer. This argument advanced by Croiset was held by such men as Van Leeuwen and Cauer to be unanswerable and it was the main support of Croiset in declaring that unity of authorship was impossible. In the first edition of his *Histoire de la littérature grecque* he said that the Iliad had but thirty-nine abstract nouns in ίη, τύς, σύνη, while the Odyssey had eighty-one. This difference between thirty-nine and eighty-one could show nothing else than the development of many generations and would make unity of authorship frankly impossible. This argument was seized upon by the advanced critics as final, and that decision could hardly be questioned, if the facts offered by Croiset[9] were really facts.

There was no appeal except to Homer and, to my great surprise, I found the figures given by Croiset for the Iliad must be exactly doubled, since the Iliad had not thirty-nine but really had seventy-eight of these abstracts. Croiset simply published his figures, he did not name the abstracts or where they were found; but in the reply to his statistics each abstract was named with the book and verse in which it was found.[10] In these years no one has questioned the truth of my statement that the Iliad has seventy-eight abstracts, or just twice the number given by Croiset. Professor Bolling, an unusually accu-

[9] In a later edition Croiset raised the number from 39 to 58.
[10] "The Relative Antiquity of the Iliad and the Odyssey Tested by Abstract Nouns," *Classical Review,* XXIV, 8 ff.

rate scholar, has tested my figures with the desire
to destroy them, but instead has confirmed them.
He tries to acquit Croiset by assuming ''errors
in counting,'' ''a moment of forgetfulness,''
''haplography led to the error,'' and the cool
assumption that Croiset meant only certain books
and not the entire Iliad, despite the fact that he
permitted himself to be quoted by all the critics
as comparing the entire Iliad and the entire
Odyssey, and also despite the fact that my article
was republished by German and French period-
icals and Croiset never made any such defense.
Professor Bolling agrees, however, in the very
manner of his apology for these errors, that
Croiset's figures are wrong, that the Iliad has
not thirty-nine but seventy-eight abstracts, and
that these two poems show a similarity in the
number of abstracts which can hardly be explained except by unity of authorship.

The arguments based on the development of
the abstract from the adjective and the proof that
certain abstracts appear only in the Odyssey,
while the adjectives from which they are derived
are found in the Iliad, seem most convincing.
Both poems are in the same position in this regard, and there are many abstracts used only
in the Iliad which are derived from adjectives
found only in the Odyssey. The following
abstracts are found only in the Iliad, the adjectives from which they are derived occur only in
the Odyssey: ἡλικίη, μνημοσύνη, ἰδρείη, κατηφείη;

and the list might be much extended. This shows
how impossible it is to date a word from its first
appearance, since the adjectives from which these
abstracts are derived must have been known to
the poet of the Iliad. Croiset in his work on
Homer discussed certain obsolescent phrases,
saying that the phrase, ἠΰς τε μέγας τε, is found
in the Iliad twenty-five times, in the Odyssey but
three, though in fact it is found in the Iliad but
eight times, in the Odyssey but once. It is almost
pathetic to know that Croiset in his long chapter
devoted to showing the linguistic differences between the Iliad and the Odyssey gave definite
figures but twice, and both absolutely wrong, for
the phrase which he said is used in the Iliad
twenty-five times is used but eight, and the
abstracts which he said are found in that poem
but thirty-nine times are found seventy-eight
times. If both these figures were too small, it
would be an easy matter to say that he did not
count certain books or certain verses; then just
enough could be omitted to get the necessary
number, but when the figures are in one case too
small and in the other over three times too large,
it is not so easy to offer a satisfying solution.

In such matters the test of language is the
real test, especially the use of words which might
escape the notice of the imitator—little unob-
trusive words. Such a word is the definite article,
ὀ, ἠ ,τό, both because it is used so frequently, and
also because it shows in Homer all the different

stages through which it passed in changing from
a pure demonstrative to a simple defining article.
The demonstrative is the older, the article the
later development. In Latin the demonstrative
ille remained a demonstrative, while in languages
derived from the Latin, as the French and the
Italian, the articular use of *il* and *le* has been
developed from the older *ille*. If the demonstrative use is predominant in certain books of Homer
and the articular in others, then the belief is
justified that these books were written at different
periods, and if the divergence be sufficiently great
they must have been written by different poets,
also.

The use of the definite article has furnished
one of the chief arguments for the comparative
lateness of the Odyssey. Monro in his *Odyssey*
II, 332, says: "The defining article is much more
frequent in the Odyssey." The use and extension
of the definite article has lately been the subject
of repeated investigation, the results of which
are in such substantial agreement that their
approximate accuracy cannot be doubted. Koch,
De Articulo Homerico (Leipzig, 1872), published
a complete list of all the examples of ὁ, ἡ, τό
in Homer, noting whether used as demonstrative
pronoun, relative pronoun, or as a defining article.
He gave no figures, but by adding up his various
lists I found that he assigned 422 examples of the
definite article to the Iliad, and 214 to the Odyssey,
that is, he put about twice as many in his list from

the Iliad as he did in his list from the Odyssey. Miss F. Melian Stawell in the Appendix to *Homer and the Iliad* published statistics for the use of the article which closely agree with those of Koch.

Stummer, *Ueber den Artikel bei Homer* (Schweinfurt, 1886), written under the guidance of von Christ, made an effort to support Christ's theory of an original Iliad and was very thorough. Stummer believed in a more restricted use of the definite article than either of the others I have named and assigned to a place among demonstrative pronouns many of the examples given as definite articles. The definite article is found in the Iliad 218 times, against Koch's 422; in the Odyssey 171 times, against Koch's 214. However, they agree in this, that they both assign the greater number to the Iliad. Stummer tried to fit his statistics into the theory of Christ, and obtained the following: number of verses in the original Iliad 8981; example of definite article in original Iliad 125, that is, one definite article in each 72 verses; verses in addition to the Iliad 6712; examples of definite article in the additions to the Iliad 93, or one definite article to each 72 verses. That is the original Iliad and the additions show exactly the same ratio in the use of the definite article. No wonder poor Stummer felt his pamphlet was a failure, and the disappointed reviewer (Bursian's *Jahresbericht* XLVI, 189), said: "The results of this investigation have not the importance one would have been inclined to expect."

To continue with the figures given by Stummer: entire Iliad 15,693 verses, 218 examples of
the definite article, or one in each 72 verses;
entire Odyssey 12,110 verses, 171 examples of
the definite article, or one to each 71 verses. In
the entire Iliad ὁ is used as a demonstrative pronoun nearly 3000 times, as a definite article 218
times, or in a ratio of 14:1; in the Odyssey, as
a demonstrative pronoun 2178 times, as a definite
article 171 times, or in a ratio of 13:1. The three
poems assigned to Hesiod have 2330 verses; the
definite article is found in Hesiod 62 times, that
is, once in each 38 verses. This word is found
in Hesiod as a demonstrative pronoun 404 times,
as a true definite article 62 times, or in a ratio
of 7:1. In the five greater Homeric Hymns there
are 1914 verses, with 57 examples of the definite
article, or one in each 33 verses; and this word
is used as a demonstrative pronoun 217 times and
as a true definite article 57 times, that is in a ratio
of 4:1. To restate these important facts in a
brief summary: The Iliad has one definite article
to each 72 verses; the Odyssey, one definite article
to each 71 verses; Hesiod, one definite article
to each 38 verses; Homeric Hymns, one definite
article to each 33 verses. Ratio of the use of the
demonstrative pronoun to the ratio of the definite
article: Iliad 14:1; Odyssey 13:1; Hesiod 7:1;
Homeric Hymns 4:1. It must be remembered that
Hesiod and the Homeric Hymns were written in
the same verse and the same dialect as the Iliad

and the Odyssey, so that this change in the use of the article must have been an unconscious change.

There could be no more cogent reason than these statistics for assigning the Iliad and the Odyssey to a single period, a period widely separated from the time of the origin of the poetry of Hesiod and of the Homeric Hymns. Such was the spell or pall cast by disintegrating criticism that Stummer, Christ, and the rest coldly passed by these important facts and saw nothing in them but a failure to reach anything of value. From the above figures it is clear that the distance from Homer to Hesiod is many times greater than the distance from Hesiod to the Homeric Hymns; and the slight advance from the Iliad to the Odyssey is just what would fall in the life of one man.

Not only is it impossible to separate the Iliad from the Odyssey on the basis of the definite article; but no strata can be thus defined within the poems themselves, else the first and the last books of the Odyssey, the two books most confidently regarded as late by the critics, would be the oldest, since they show the most restricted use of the definite article.

Dr. Shewan[11] has found that the short forms of the dative plural, that is, αις, οις, ης, instead of αισι, οισι, ησι, occur in the Iliad and the Odyssey but once in each 240 verses; in Hesiod and in the Homeric Hymns these short forms occur once in

[11] *The Lay of Dolon,* 52.

each thirty-six verses. Doctor Shewan also found
by testing typical books of the Iliad that the cases
where the diphthong must be read in the genitive
ending of the second declension, a supposedly
later ending, occurs once in each sixty verses in
A and in K, while in Hesiod and the Homeric
Hymns such a genitive is found once in each
nineteen verses.

Monro, *Homeric Grammar,* 344, says: "Neglect
of position is perceptibly commoner in the Odyssey
than in the Iliad." By neglect of position is
meant the scansion of a vowel as short before a
mute consonant and a liquid. Doctor Shewan[12]
has made a list of all these metrical defects and
finds that there are twenty-nine examples in the
Iliad and but twenty in the Odyssey—numbers
which closely correspond with the relative size of
the two poems. He found also that these defects
occur relatively five times as often in Hesiod and
the Homeric Hymns as they occur in the Iliad
and the Odyssey. I have tested the work done
by Doctor Shewan again and again, and I have
always found it absolutely reliable.

This remarkable agreement of the Iliad and
the Odyssey in these small but important linguistic matters in contrast with the changes
found in Hesiod and the Homeric Hymns can have
but one explanation; they belong to the same age.

The Greeks developed in their own language
after they had separated from the Indo-European
stock a perfect in *κα*, the existing Greek literature

12 *Idem,* 108.

showing the clear development of these perfects
from a sparing use in the third singular indica-
tive to a wide use in the other moods. If certain
books in Homer show free use of this perfect
while others do not, then we have at hand an easy
test of their relative antiquity. Such a test has
not escaped the service of the critics, but it has
not been useful, since the Iliad has seventeen such
perfects, the Odyssey thirteen. The thirteen of
the Odyssey bear about the same ratio to the
seventeen of the Iliad as the number of verses
of the Odyssey bears to the number of the Iliad,
so that the Iliad has one perfect in κα to each 923
verses, the Odyssey one to each 931 verses. The
two poems belong to the same period in a perfectly well-defined stage in the development of
this perfect.[13]

Professor Jebb in his tests of the difference
between the Iliad and the Odyssey said: ''Hiatus
in the bucolic dieresis is about twice as frequent
in the Iliad as in the Odyssey.''[14] By this he
means that a word ends in a vowel and the following word begins with a vowel at the end of
the fourth foot about twice as often in the Odyssey
as in the Iliad. The fact is that the Iliad has sixty
examples of this hiatus, the Odyssey sixty-six,
that is, the two poems have 126 and they are so
evenly distributed that if three are taken from
the one and added to the other they will have

[13] A complete discussion of these perfects is found in *Class.
Phil.*, VI, 159 ff.
[14] Jebb, *Homer*, ed. 5, 139.

an identical number. Miss Stawell and I have independently counted these examples and have reached the same conclusion.[15] This agreement is surprising, even if it had not been an argument of higher criticism that the difference is so great as to make unity of authorship impossible. Jebb also added that "books xxiii and xxiv share with the Odyssey this free use of the hiatus." However the fact is that O has eight examples of this hiatus, E has seven, B has six, Λ has five, but Ψ has only four, and is thus in fifth place, and Ω and T are tied for the ninth place. One of the easiest suppositions of the destructive critics is that no one will defend certain books of the Iliad, so that in discussing these books facts are hardly considered necessary.

Jebb also cites the adjectival use of οὐδέν as being characteristic of the Odyssey,[16] yet there is but a solitary example of this use in the Odyssey (δ 350) and that extremely doubtful. The Iliad has two perfectly clear examples, K 216, X 518; but in the face of this, the adjectival use of the negative, which is unambiguous only in the Iliad, is selected as being a peculiar mark of the Odyssey. This is of a piece with the argument of the early chorizontes, who said that προπάροιθεν in a temporal sense is found only in the Odyssey; whereas in fact the Iliad has several examples of this temporal use, K 476, Λ 734, X 197, while there

[15] *Homer and the Iliad,* 317.
[16] *Homer,* 188.

seems to be but one example in the Odyssey, λ 483.
This use is discussed by Leaf in his note to K 476.

It is agreed that back of the poetry of Homer
there must have been songs in the Aeolic dialect,
for traces of this Aeolic dialect are in all parts
of Homer. A fairly easy test of the antiquity of
Homeric books might be furnished by the measure
of predominance of these early forms, and it is
well-known that Fick and others have by this test
tried to select an original Iliad and an original
Odyssey. No test would seem to be more convincing than the comparative frequency of the
occurrences of the Aeolic infinitive in -έμεν. It
is not found in Ionic-Attic Greek, Homeric poetry
having inherited it from earlier songs.

Witte, in an article on the Homeric language
in *Pauly-Wissowa,* has shown that the Homeric
verse has a peculiarly conservative influence just
before the bucolic dieresis, and adds that Bekker
has observed that in this place in the verse the
Iliad has 116 infinitives in -έμεν, the Odyssey but
fifty-one. This great difference can hardly be
explained by difference in theme, and it must be
admitted that the poet of the Odyssey has here
betrayed his comparative lateness, if the figures
given above are correct.

Bekker is known as one of the outstanding
Homeric scholars of the last century; and as he
is editor of one of the most illustrious recensions
of the Iliad and the Odyssey, we are fortunately
able to test his figures in the readings of his own

text. His statistics for the Iliad are substantially correct; in reading the Iliad in search of these infinitives I found 114, as compared with his 116, and I might easily have overlooked two; but in a like search in his own edition of the Odyssey I found, not his fifty-one—I actually found seventy,[17] so that, though his figures for the Iliad are essentially correct, those in the Odyssey must be increased nearly forty per cent. Inasmuch as the Iliad has 3583 more verses than the Odyssey, the seventy examples of the Odyssey show little relative decline, when compared with the 116 of the longer poem.

When we compare this usage of the Iliad and the Odyssey with that of the Homeric Hymns we find the greatest contrast, for these hymns have this archaic infinitive before the bucolic dieresis but once in each one thousand verses, while the first four books of the Odyssey have one in each one hundred verses. Evidently this form was but a learned survival in the age when the Homeric hymns were created and many years must have separated them from the era which produced the Iliad and the Odyssey, whereas the identical treatment as revealed in these two great poems assigns them to a single epoch.

The epic poet often honored a man by calling him not by his own name but by the name of his father, so that Agamemnon is often called Atreides, Achilles is called Peleides, and Odysseus

[17] All the examples of these infinitives are given in *Class. Phil.* XIV, 137.

is called Laertiades. Wilhelm Meyer wrote a dissertation on the use of the Homeric patronymics[18] which was at once hailed as a classic by the higher critics. (In 1907 there were no credited Homeric critics other than higher critics.) Meyer's results as given in his own summary are briefly as follows: "The patronymics grow rarer not only in the later portions of the Iliad, but also in all parts of the Odyssey. From this decreasing use of the patronymic it is evident that there must have been an interval of many years between the composition of these two poems." When I answered this article (*Class. Phil.* VII, 293), I explained the difference in numbers in the use of the patronymic as due to the greater preponderance of heroes in the Iliad and to the fact that so many characters in the Odyssey are ignoble or commonplace, hence the greater number in the Iliad is to be expected. Even this explanation is entirely unnecessary, for the markedly decreasing use of the patronymics in the assumedly late books is pure fiction, as this simple test will show.

The two books which Meyer regarded as belonging to the oldest stratum are A and X. The following men who appear in A have patronymics: Achilles, Calchas, Agamemnon, Menelaus, and Patroclus, five in all. The following heroes in X have patronymics: Achilles, Agamemnon, Menelaus, and Priam, or four in all. Of those which appear in X only one is not found in A, so that

[18] *De Homeri Patronymicis*, Göttingen, 1907.

but six of the men who appear in these two books have patronymics. These two books have a combined length of 1126 verses.

The book which all the critics put as the latest and the worst in Homer is the last book of the Odyssey. In this last book of the Odyssey the following men are mentioned with the honoring patronymic: Achilles, Agamemnon, Laertes, Odysseus, Patroclus, Apheidas, and Halitherses, or seven in all. Hence these 548 verses of ω have one more patronymic than are found in the 1126 combined verses of A and X.

A test applied to the first book of the Odyssey, another book which the critics have regarded as late, shows that it has the following patronymics: Atreides, Agamemnonides, Mermerides, and Peisenorides, only one of which is found in the Iliad. This book in 444 verses has but one less patronymic than A has in 611, and exactly the same as X in 515 verses. Furthermore two of the patronymics found in α are found only there, though each of the patronymics of X is found in many books of the Iliad.

One is not obliged to explain the alleged change between the Iliad and the Odyssey; all he needs to do is to count the number of patronymics. No other discussion of this vaunted treatise is necessary, for it is absolutely at variance with easily tested facts. How could any scholar write such an article? How could competent professors accept it with the very highest praise? How could editors and scholars receive it as a final and authoritative contribution to human knowledge? Yet it is on the basis of just such facts as these that Huxley believed the critics had scientifically demonstrated that the Iliad and the Odyssey could not be by a single poet.

I have never taken up the investigation of any assumedly important difference between the language of the Iliad and the Odyssey and found that the underlying statements were true. I do not regard as of any importance the fact that the Iliad mentions beans and the Odyssey does not, or that words for wounds and wounding abound in the Iliad, while they are rarely or never used in the Odyssey. The observation that the Iliad has more references to storms, snows, and the phenomena of heaven, an observation which was hailed by the critics as if it were the discovery of a new planet, made little impression on me, so little that I did not answer the argument when it first appeared, because the answer was so easy that I thought the writer thereof would see it and receive the credit of retraction without outside suggestion; but the author did not see that the reason for the fewer references in the Odyssey is because the action of that poem is mostly under roof, while the Iliad and its setting are out of doors, with warriors in the field. We move in the Odyssey from palace to palace, first in Ithaca, then in Pylos, then in Sparta, and then back to Ithaca. Nature withdraws as we stand under

cover, and the average person learns more of
the phenomena of heaven in one week's camping
than in an entire lifetime in the city. Weather
is only an incident in towns, but it governs everything in the tent and field. The less frequent
references to the phenomena of heaven do not
show any less "sensibility to natural phenomena"
but do show that Homer knew that storms, clouds,
and the sky mean more to men living in camps
or in the fields than they do to inhabitants of the
towns.

These and a hundred other similar differences
which must exist between poems of different or
similar themes, even by the same poet, are of no
importance. The real tests. are found in the
hidden matters of meter, digamma, abstract
nouns, patronymics, Aeolic forms, formations of
the perfect, hiatus, case endings, and such unconscious indications of the poet's land and age. All
these proofs once widely accepted as sufficient evidence of diverse authorship have utterly broken
down, because, when tested by the facts, they have
been found to rest on false assertions and false
statistics. Doctor Shewan, Miss Stawell, Professor Shorey, Professor Bassett, as well as others
in England, Germany, France, Italy, and elsewhere, have tested other phases of these so-called
proofs, and they have generally found the statistics and the assertions entirely wrong. In ten
years no higher critic has tried to reëstablish one
of these demolished arguments. The only counter

attack is a feeble remonstrance that, although the
assertions we have attacked are false, perhaps
these errors may have sprung up in some other
way; thus the critics hope to shift the attack and
to set up a new science which will not expose the
errors of higher criticism, but will waste itself
in discussion of the genesis of these errors. We
are only remotely interested in the way these
errors arose; all we desire is the admission that
they are errors, and that Homer has been unjustly
attacked.

So long as the critics assumed a superior attitude and remained in the clouds and said: "We
can feel here the great difference from the old
epic," "Here we can detect the ring of the old
epic coin," or "He who cannot grasp this fact,
should not busy himself with epic poetry, for he
is incompetent to understand"—no one dared
to show his lack of any true aesthetic feeling by
venturing to doubt them. Such critics needed to
present no evidence, for, as Cicero says in his
Tusc. Disp. i, 49, "Who, although they present no
arguments, could yet crush us by their very
authority." *Qui ut rationem nullam adferrent,
ipsa auctoritate nos frangerent.* But when they
grew impatient at staying in the clouds and
began to present facts and figures, then we could
test their assertions and examine their evidence.
Higher criticism committed suicide when it
fretted at being a cult and aspired to become a
science.

The pretenses of the critics seem such a sham that one wonders if after all they are not speaking in some cipher, some hidden code, so that when they say six they mean fourteen, when they say nine they mean five, and so for all their other facts and figures. Then, of course, what they mean was never to be detected from that which they say, and all our labor has been wasted labor, and they have inwardly laughed at our discomfiture. It is only on the basis of some cryptogram that I can explain Gilbert Murray's theory[19] that the Homeric Greeks were men under a vow of sexual chastity, since next to fighting their greatest efforts were spent in breaking any such vows; or Thomson's theory of expurgation,[20] based on the assumption that Homer has not a trace of the envy of the gods. Does not Menelaus complain that it was the envy of the gods which had prevented him and Odysseus from spending their old age together? Does not Penelope lament that it was divine envy which had taken away her husband in her youth? I can offer no other explanation of Menrad's attempt[21] to show that Odysseus was a sun-god. Menrad says: "The twelve companions who went with Odysseus to explore and visit the haunts of Circe were the twelve months." Yet Homer definitely fixes the number at forty-five! Menrad says, "the 118 suitors are the 118 days of the winter months,"

19 *Rise of Greek Epic*, 152.
20 *Studies in the Odyssey*, 11.
21 *Der Urmythus der Odyssee*, 26, 42.

but Homer explicitly tells us that there were 108 suitors. How did he get these figures? Had he never read Homer, or did he use some cryptogram from a hidden cipher? Or is scholarship so limp a thing that facts are nothing and one may substitute anything one chooses for anything that is?

Saddest of all is the fact that, for about a century, Homeric criticism has lived apart from Homer. Each new theory is accepted as an addition to human knowledge, with no attempt to test it by the evidence of the poems themselves. The best possible proof that higher critics have made no real study of Homer is furnished by the fact that not a single one of them has ever independently detected any of the errors to which I have called attention above.

Van Leeuwen, the great Hellenist of Holland and for a generation one of the leading destructive critics of Homer, just as he was laying down his life's work, wrote these pathetic words (*Mnemosyne,* 1910, 341):

I recognize the error in which I have long been involved, since now I see the better way. The fault was in our teachers who taught us the things they thought were true, which we in turn presented to our pupils. I now proclaim openly my belief. The context of the Iliad and the Odyssey cannot be loosed without the ruin of the whole. Each is a single poem, conceived, elaborated, composed by a single poet. The poetry of Homer will continue to live so long as we permit it to remain entire, but it will die, pass away, and slip through our fingers, if we undertake to dissect it or to tear it apart.

Roemer in his last work, *Homerische Aufsätze,* published in his seventieth year, said, "Most men who have spent their lives with Homer have never given Homer a chance." That is the simple truth; Homer has not been given a chance and most students who have done work on Homer have been directed to find errors and contradictions where none exist. These disintegrating arguments, based on false statistics, have been wax in the ears of nearly all students of Homer. Their ears have never had a chance to catch the music of his songs; they have been as deaf to the voice of Homer as were the companions of Odysseus to the voice of the Sirens.

The linguistic attack on Homer, the most serious that could be devised, has entirely failed to create a presumption of diverse authorship. Instead, this attack has made it most improbable that two poems of such great length could show such practical identity of language, unless they were the creation of a single age and of a single poet.

CHAPTER IV

THE ANTIQUITIES AND KINDRED MATTERS

The assumed differences in language have furnished the chief argument for the modern chorizontes, but this argument has been supported on all sides by the assumption of differences or contradictions in geography, topography, chronology, customs, religion, government, and the greatest divergences of every sort. The list is formidable and apparently overwhelming. These differences were assumed to prove not only that the Iliad and the Odyssey were not the work of a single poet but that each poem was itself made up of a mass of individual and contradictory songs.

Professor Rothe's recent book in defense of the unity of the Odyssey, *Die Odyssee als Dichtung,* was supposedly crushed by the unanswerable arguments presented by Finsler and Wilamowitz, that the first four books of the Odyssey demand as their background the heat of summer, although the story of Odysseus from his arrival in the land of the Phaeacians until his reunion with Penelope demands the cold and raw temperature of the late autumn and early winter. The whole story of the Odyssey covers only about forty days.

If part of it assumes as its setting the heat of
summer and the rest the cold of early winter it
would obviously be impossible to embrace both
these seasons in a space of forty days. The poets
of the Odyssey have thus betrayed themselves by
these careless references, and the poem in its
present form must be an amalgamation of at least
two poems, one with the setting of summer, the
other with the setting of winter.

It is manifestly difficult to assign such poetry
to definite months or seasons, yet the Odyssey
does presuppose a background in the seasons of
the year. Of this there are several indefinite indications and one that is supposedly definite.

The definite indication is as follows: When
Odysseus (ε 272) went from the presence of
Calypso and sailed toward the land of the Phaeacians, he guided his course by the Pleiades, the
late-setting Boötes, and the Bear. The Bear is
visible every night of the year, so that its presence
gives no indication of the season. The Pleiades
and Boötes, however, are changeable, hence the
fact that they were both visible should give a
rough notion of the time of the year. The German scholars named above said that this reference
could be to the winter season only, since, they
argued, it was not until late autumn that the
Pleiades and Boötes could both be seen at the
same time.

Professor Fox, director of the Dearborn Astronomical Observatory, has very kindly figured for

me the exact position of these stars from 900 to 700 B.C. His figures are for latitude 39° N. This is the latitude of Smyrna, the assumed home of Homer, and the approximate latitude of Corcyra, the conjectural home of the Phaeacians. Since Odysseus sailed, keeping these stars on his left, that is, in an easterly direction, we may presume that that latitude would not be amiss for the home of Calypso, as well as for that of Homer, Alcinous, and Odysseus.

Professor Fox's conclusions are as follows:

After allowing for the precession of the equinoxes it is found that in 800 B.C. the Pleiades were visible in lat. 39° N. from dusk to dawn, that is all night, from September 1 to November 2; also that Arcturus, the essential star in the constellation Boötes, set during the hours of daylight, except during the period extending from June 15 to October 21. If a sailor saw during the same night the Pleiades and the setting of Boötes, the earliest date must have been September 1, the latest October 21. The change in season of these stars since 800 B.C., because of the precession of the equinoxes, is about thirty-one days, so that these conditions would now fall about one month later in lat. 39° N., with a corresponding lengthening of the period as the observer moves north.

If it was the setting of Boötes which attracted the hero's attention, and if this setting could not be seen later than October 21, then it is impossible to assign this voyage to a later season in the year, and the cool assumption that these stars demanded the late autumn is thus absolutely false. How did such an error arise? Here again my astronomical friend gave me complete satisfaction. Owing to the precession of the equinoxes, the constellations are delayed about a day per century; also the farther north one goes, the later these northern constellations sink from view, so that in Berlin the setting of Boötes may now be seen as late as the twenty-fifth of November, and the rising of the Pleiades has grown correspondingly later. Finsler and Wilamowitz assumed that Odysseus was a contemporary sailing in the latitude of Berlin! The statement, then, that the movements of Odysseus must fall in the late autumn is absolutely false.

No better is the other assertion that the journey of Telemachus demands the heat of summer. The trip made by Telemachus was from Ithaca to Pylos and on to Sparta. Ithaca lies south of lat. 39° N. and is thus about 150 miles south of Naples, and the climate differs but little from that of the nearby Corfu. Baedeker, in his *Greece*, 252, says of the climate of Corfu: "The temperature is mild in October and the first half of November, but June, July, August and (often) September are very hot." The last week of September, to which I assign this journey, would be just the season when the heat of summer has begun to yield to the coolness of autumn. There is but one reference in regard to the temperature in the first book of the Odyssey (443), where it is said the young man slept covered with wool. The fact that he was thus covered shows that we are not dealing with the heat of summer, but with the coolness of early autumn. From Ithaca he went to Pylos, which is supposed to have been on or near the site of the modern Navarino, the climate of which is thus described by Mr. Grundy in his well-known book, *The Great Persian War,* VIII: "During the four weeks I spent at Navarino the thermometer never fell below 93° Fahrenheit, night or day, and rose to 110° or 112° in the absolute darkness of a closed house at midday." In the evening, when Telemachus started to go to his ship, as if to spend the night there, Nestor was highly indignant, protesting that he had sufficient coverings to keep not only his family, but his guests warm and snug. If the weather were the summer weather described by Mr. Grundy, then these words about a bountiful supply of coverlets were intended as a piece of dry humor, a quality alien to the character of Nestor. When Telemachus and his companion started on their trip to Sparta, they whipped their horses, and their horses were so eager to go that they did not rest at any period of the day, but kept right on. During the long, hot days of summer they could not have traveled all day, but must have rested during the heat of noon, and limited their going to the cool hours, if there were any cool hours, of the morning and evening. These verses (γ 484 ff.) show that the theory of these critics was not founded on the Odyssey, but was an independent conjecture, which ignored not only the more difficult facts of astronomy but the easily ascertainable statements of the poem.[1]

In the second half of the last century skepticism had full control of all phases of Homer, so that not only the poet had been eliminated but his Troy also had been relegated to the realm of the impossible. Homer described that city as near the sea, on a low hill, close to two rivers. From this city Mount Ida could be seen in one direction and the island, Samothrace, in the other. Hardly more than fifty years ago it was agreed that no such city had existed near the shore, that it was impossible for any magnificent civilization to have arisen in that early day in the Troad, and that the bulk of the Iliad was the magnified tradition of a stronghold on a spur of Mount Ida, far from the Dardanelles. Thus, practically ignoring the Iliad, it was believed that the "mighty Ilium rising from the plain," was only the confused picture of an unimposing fortress back among the hills. This belief was so thoroughly established that in practically all the classical atlases, except the very recent, Troy is marked on the maps as definitely located on this un-Homeric site, the modern village of Bunarbaschi.

At the period of the greatest Homeric agnosticism a German merchant, Heinrich Schliemann, who had accumulated a fortune by the time he had reached early middle life, took up the study of Greek in order that he might read Homer in the

[1] "Assumed Contradictions in the Seasons of the Odyssey," *Class. Phil.* XI, 148.

poet's own language. He not only read Homer but committed much of him to memory as well, and in his enthusiasm visited the plain of Troy. He was utterly regardless and perhaps ignorant of the arguments of the critics and started to search for the site of the old city, using Homer for his guide in the safe confidence with which a mariner turns to his compass and his charts. In the face of the united ridicule of the learned classical world, and in spite of difficulties apparently unsurmountable, he found a city on the very spot where Homer had placed it and just such a city as Homer had described. Never has simple faith been better justified and better rewarded. Few of his original critics were convinced, but they are all dead and their writings have joined in their fate. I am familiar with the name of no scholar, under seventy years of age, who doubts that Schliemann has discovered the ruins of the very city whose fate inspired the poetry of Homer. Schliemann was aided in finding the site of Troy by Frank Calvert, consular representative of Great Britain and the United States at the Dardanelles, who had already started to excavate at Hissarlik when Schliemann was searching elsewhere.

Doctor Walter Leaf in his edition of the Iliad was one of the most eager followers of the doctrines of destructive criticism and believed that the topographical contradictions in regard to the Troad made the unity of the Iliad impossible.

In his note to E 355 he wrote: "However it has been shown by Hercher that it is impossible to reconcile Homeric geographical statements with themselves or with each other." He wrote that sentence at a time when he trusted the opinions of others. Later he visited Troy and studied the ruins and the topography of all that district with a thoroughness rarely equaled, comparing each part of the city and of the plain with the words of the poem. After this careful and independent investigation on the spot and with Homer in his hand he wrote: "One thing at least has passed from me beyond all doubt; the poet has put into living words a tradition founded on real fighting in this very place." . . . . "It is a remarkable fact that, so far as I can judge, no case of local inconsistency, not a single anatopism, can be brought home to the Iliad."[2]

The second book of the Iliad closes with two catalogues, first a fairly full catalogue of the Greeks, then a very meager catalogue of the Trojans. This Trojan Catalogue is perhaps the least esteemed part of Homer. Doctor Leaf, in his *Iliad,* said of it: "The Catalogue of the Trojans differs notably from that of the Greeks in the evident want of detailed knowledge of the countries with which it deals." When he had visited the regions from which the Trojans and their allies had come, however, he wrote thus: "The Trojan Catalogue, in particular, seems to represent accurately a state of things which must

[2] *Troy, A Study in Homeric Geography,* 169, 12.

have existed at the time of the Trojan War, and could not have existed after it, nor for long before'' (p. 13); ''The result of my journey was to confirm the view that the Troad, so far as it is described in the Iliad, is described from true historical knowledge, and that so much of the Trojan Catalogue as deals with the kingdom of Priam may be taken as an authentic historical document: a conclusion which I do not hesitate to extend to the larger part which tells of the Trojan allies'' (p. 6). These words were written by the man who had done more than any other man in England to spread the separatists' doctrines, but written when he had turned his eyes from the critics and looked at things as they are.

Arguments from language are settled neither by presumptions nor by reasonings, but solely by a study of the poems themselves, and Doctor Leaf's investigation on the spot seems conclusive to me, especially as he went to Troy after he had already published his belief in the topographical ignorance of Homer.

The vanity of all other methods is shown in the fact that Robert[3] argues that the location of the city of Troy was accurately given only in the oldest parts of the Iliad, yet Wilamowitz with equal assurance and with similar logic asserts that the location of Ilium was unknown in the oldest parts of the Iliad, and any accurate topographical indication is a sure mark of lateness:

[3] ''Topographische Probleme der Ilias,'' *Hermes* XLII, 78.

"The poet of the Iliad had absolutely no conception of the location of the city of Troy."[4] Yet Schliemann and Calvert took that same Iliad and with it as their sole guide found Troy, and Doctor Leaf, an avowed skeptic, when he read that Iliad in the plains of Troy and studied the ruins, renounced his doubts.

The leader of the Greeks was given as Agamemnon from Mycenae. Mycenae was situated on the edge of a rugged plain in the lower foothills, a good day's march from Corinth. In history it appears only as a miserable little village, able to furnish but eighty men to meet the invading army of Xerxes; and Mycenae and Tiryns, with the adjoining districts, could provide but four hundred troops for the great struggle at Plataea. How feeble their combined strength then was is shown by the fact that Phlius furnished for that one battle a full thousand men and Sicyon three thousand. Homer pictured Mycenae as "rich in gold," "well-built," the center of a vast empire whose ruler could muster an army of over one hundred thousand men, who controlled twelve hundred ships, and who was so firmly established in his power that he could hold this army together in a foreign field without a decisive victory.

Mycenae is hardly mentioned in any history of fifty years ago, as it was not imagined that such a city as that pictured in Homer had ever

4 *Die Ilias und Homer*, 333.

existed, and the whole story was hardly deemed worthy of a denial. There was also a vague tradition that Agamemnon and others of his family had been buried there. Schliemann, with his wonderful capacity for accepting as true any essential statement in Homer, began excavations in Mycenae. He chanced to begin digging in just the right spot and soon found gravestones, then the graves themselves. In these graves were skeletons literally buried in gold, crowns, scepters, bracelets, plates, and jars; some of these weighing sixty ounces of solid gold. In one of these graves were found seven hundred discs of gold and twenty-four enormous breastpins; in another were many artistic swords of bronze and gold. The faces of some of the dead were portrayed by golden masks. Evidently Homer was not far wrong when he described Mycenae as "rich in gold" and when he made it the center of a great and wealthy empire.

The walls and the general culture of Troy and Mycenae so closely correspond that there is no doubt that they were flourishing at the same period, a period which has been named the Mycenaean Age. It was this age which furnished the background for the Homeric poems, and the civilization pictured by Homer roughly agrees with the civilization recorded on the monuments and the discoveries connected with the end of the Mycenaean period. Back of this Mycenaean Age is an earlier powerful civilization centering in

Crete, but the Homeric picture is of the Mycenaean civilization near the period of its collapse, about 1100 B.C.

Many verses which were supposed by the critics to represent customs arising later than Homer are now seen to describe things known in the Mycenaean Age. In K 173 a razor is mentioned, the only reference to this instrument in Homer. This was therefore seized upon as a sure proof of the lateness of this book, for the use of razors was assumed to be comparatively late; but a razor has been found in a grave in Mycenae, proving that razors were in use long before Homer. The Iliad and the Odyssey have but a single reference to slings (N 600) and once a reference is made to "the well-twisted threads from the fleece of the sheep" (N 716), where a sling is probably meant. These two passages have been ruthlessly removed as later additions, but a fragment of a silver vase found in Mycenae represents a group of slingers near a wall hurling missiles at a besieging foe.

An attempt was made to divide the books of Homer on the basis of the armor, since it was assumed that in the oldest portions the warrior used only a great shield which protected the entire body. It was argued that this great shield so completely shielded the body that no other protecting armor was necessary, hence all references to coats of mail or cuirasses were to be regarded as later additions. It was on the basis of the armor that Robert tried to reconstruct his original Iliad, rejecting all verses or scenes which referred to small shields or coats of mail.

No such uniformity of armor ever existed among the Greeks, and in the Mycenaean representations of huntsmen and warriors the variations in styles of armor are quite as great as in the verses of Homer. In the famous Warrior Vase the soldiers all have small shields extending only from the shoulder to the hip, and they seem to have a protection for their body much like a coat of mail.[5] In the inlaid dagger blade the shields cover the entire body,[6] and in the silver fragment, which represents the slingers, the shields seem to extend to just below the hip. In an early Cretan seal the warrior clearly has a protection under his shield, that is, he depends on both the shield and the coat of mail.[7] All these various representations of armor found in early monuments show that the descriptions of armor in Homer are no more varied than the armor pictured from life.

The assumed difficulties and contradictions in the descriptions of Homeric palaces have all been cleared up and harmony found by the recovery of the actual foundations of just such palaces.[8] No test by which it has been sought to separate the Iliad and the Odyssey or any part of either

[5] Fowler and Wheeler, *Greek Archaeology*, 90.
[6] *Idem*, 77.
[7] *Anthropology and the Classics*, 57.
[8] Bassett, ''The Palace of Odysseus,'' *Am. Jour. of Archaeology*, 1919, 288 ff.

poem has found confirmation or support in the finds made at any of the numerous Mycenaean sites.

Professor Seymour, although he did not believe in Homeric unity, could find no evidence for his want of faith when he considered the life and civilization portrayed in these two poems. In his *Life in the Homeric Age* he wrote (p. 13): "As regards these questions we are obliged to regard the Homeric poems as units. The evidence for the later date of the Odyssey as yet is philological, not archaeological." This was written in 1907, just before tests of the accuracy of these philological arguments had begun to be made. We know now that the philological evidences on which he based his belief have been totally discredited.

Modern separatists have laid great stress on the fact that the Odyssey shows a marked advance in the notions of piety and holiness, and in the words expressing these ideas. This is no proof for diverse authorship. Shakespeare in his earlier plays never uses the word "pious," though in Hamlet and subsequent plays that word is found no less than eleven times.[9] We may say of any passage of poetry that such a word or idea was used, but we cannot assume that the idea omitted or left unsaid was not known.

The poet of the Odyssey mentions the palm tree, the poet of the Iliad does not, but we cannot argue that this tree became known to the Greeks

[9] Professor Bradley, quoted by Miss Stawell, *Homer and the Iliad*, 108.

in the interval between the creation of the two poems. The Iliad mentions the grasshopper, cranes, eels, maggots, swans, sparrows, sparlings, the ass, and many other forms of common animal life which are not named in the Odyssey, yet must have been known to the author of that poem.

The Iliad has roughly 1500 words which are not found in the Odyssey but which must have been perfectly familiar to educated people at the time the Odyssey was composed. We can argue absolutely nothing from the silences of the poem, unless we have some external proof that what is not mentioned is also not known. It is a strange and a most remarkable fact that Homer never describes the setting of a ring nor carved stones, although nothing in the art of the age he is portraying is more characteristic or shows greater skill than the carving of these settings.

The fact that Homer wrote poetry as poetry, not as history, not as theology, and not as archaeology, makes it impossible to do more than roughly outline the life and the civilization of his actors. The Mycenaean finds help to fill in some of that outline but most of it remains a blank. We must exercise great caution in drawing arguments from silence or from the comparative frequency with which words are used. We know, for example, that Emerson was not acquainted with the kodak, not because he does not use that word, but because we have independent evidence that both the instrument and the word came into

being after his time, but we are not justified in
drawing a like conclusion if the word is not found
in the writings of Stephen Phillips or Alfred
Noyes.   Homeric silences similarly, when unsupported by external evidence, furnish no proof of
the poet's choice or of his knowledge.   We must
know from some outside source that Homer was
ignorant of the things he did not mention before
we can draw any important conclusions therefrom.

In the sixth book of the Iliad, 303, the women
of Troy try to win the favor of Athena by making
her an offering of a splendid garment.   Doctor
Leaf describes this image of Athena as "a rude
wooden image such as survived in many temples
into historic times."   But the critics have seen
in this image a mark not of rude antiquity but
of polished lateness, and Bethe uses this verse
with confident enthusiasm to prove[10] that the Iliad
could not have come into being until the sixth
century B.C.   He assumes that Homer was describing a seated statue of Athena of life size, and he
argues that these large statues, these life-sized
images of the gods, were not created before the
sixth century; therefore the scene in the Iliad with
its great seated image of Athena could not have
been created before the time of Solon.   There
is nothing, however, but Bethe's fancy to prove
that this image was large.   Homer makes no
reference to its size; all he says is 'Αθηναίης ἐπὶ

10 *Neue Jahrbücher f. d. cl. Phil.*, 1919, 1–16.

γούνασι. There is no reason for regarding the image of Athena as life size, and but little for regarding it as seated. The noun "knees" and the verb "take by the knees" are constantly used by Homer in a figurative sense. In Λ 130 Agamemnon overtook the sons of Antimachus, both in one chariot, who, when they saw they could not escape, took him by the knees, γουναζέσθην, begging for their lives. It would have been impossible for two men standing in a small chariot to clasp the knees of a man standing on the ground, hence the verb must have been used in a figurative sense. The common phrase, "these things lie on the knees of the gods," θεῶν ἐν γούνασι κεῖται, could hardly be forced to mean that all the gods were conceived as always remaining seated. It was simply used to mean, "These things are now out of our control and are in the keeping of the gods." This is all the phrase need mean in regard to the image of Athena, and the verse is best translated, "The robe was given over to the keeping of the goddess." We know from Strabo xiii, 601, that in historical times the image of Athena in her temple in Troy was a standing image; also the ancient coins from the vicinity of Ilium have many representations of Athena; but, so far as those coins have been reproduced in the exhaustive work of von Fritze,[11] not one represents the goddess as seated. The testimony of Strabo, the coins, and the conservatism in cult matters, all unite in proving that in

11 Appendix to Dörpfeld's *Troja und Ilion.*

Homer the goddess was not pictured as seated. Bethe's whole argument for the lateness of the Iliad rests on the assumption that life-sized and seated statues of the gods were first seen in Greece about 600 B.C., and that in Homer we have the description of such a statue; hence the passage must be at least as late as the sixth century. The argument has two serious defects: first, Homer does not give the slightest indication that the image was life-sized—that is pure presumption—and, second, the evidence clearly shows that the image was not seated.[12]

Perhaps no more convincing argument for the late date of certain portions of the Odyssey has been advanced than the argument in regard to the Sicels. The Iliad has no references to these western lands and their inhabitants, and it has been supposed that references in the Odyssey must belong to a time later than Greek colonization in southern Italy and Sicily. The argument is so simple that it is given in the handbooks as a fact, e.g. in Christ-Schmid.

We know when the first Greek settlements were made in Sicily; hence the critics had a definite date and could show that these references could not be earlier than the middle of the eighth century. However Signor Orsi has recently carried on excavations in these regions and has found that the inhabitants of Bruttium had the same stage and style of civilization as the Sicels

[12] An excellent discussion of Bethe's theory is given by Drerup, *Berliner phil. Wochenschrift*, 1919, nos. 51 and 52.

in Sicily. Moreover, what is of the very greatest importance, he found fragments of many sorts of undoubted Greek vases, fragments antedating by many centuries the oldest Greek settlements in the west, and thus proved that long before the settlers came to Italy and Sicily, Greek traders and sailors were familiar with these very regions, where they traded the artistic and useful wares of the Greeks for the copper and raw materials of the lands lying in the central basin of the Mediterranean.[13] It should not have been left to the discoveries of Signor Orsi to show that a civilization such as the Mycenaean could not have remained ignorant of these nearby lands.

It has often been observed that the Iliad has far more similes than the Odyssey, the ratio being approximately four to one, and this has been believed to prove that the poet of the Odyssey was decidedly inferior to the poet of the Iliad in this creative and visualizing power.[14] However, the reason for this disparity is evident. The Iliad has a theme most difficult to enliven and to diversify, and the constant repetition of battles and of single combats would be tedious in the extreme were the story not told with a wealth of poetic adornment. But the varied events of the Odyssey need no such embellishment, just as in the Iliad, when there is variety of theme or of action sufficient to grip for its own sake, there are few or no similes. The first book of that poem has

13 Oldfather, *Class. Weekly*, VIII, 66.
14 Finsler, *Homer*, I, 328 ff.

rapid and changing action, but it has no elaborate simile; while the second book, with the marshalling of the troops, abounds in similes. No one could argue that B shows higher poetic powers than the preceding book. In neither the Iliad nor the Odyssey are the similes used for their own sake, or for adornment, but only to hold or direct the attention of the hearer. A telling proof that the difference is due to the theme and not to the author is found in the fact that in Vergil the books of travel and of adventure have but few similes, while the fighting scenes have relatively many. Book III, which is largely Odyssean in content, has only one simile, and book XII, the book most resembling the fighting scenes of the Iliad, has eighteen similes; hence in this poem of undoubted unity we find that those parts which most nearly correspond with the story of the Odyssey have few similes, while those most resembling the action of the Iliad have them in abundance.[15] We cannot deny unity to Homer on the basis of poetic qualities which are not questioned in Vergil.

The similes of the Iliad and the Odyssey show exactly the same traits, the same partiality for the external world, the world one sees, rather than for comparisons drawn from the realm of the mind. Each poem has but one simile based on the mental world, and in each the speed of thought is the occasion of the comparison. Each poem shows the same enthusiasm and admiration

[15] Statistics for Vergil are given by Thomson, *De comparationibus Vergilianis.* See *Class. Jour.*, XIII, 687.

for lions. Oddly enough this trait was shared
by the artist who created the famous dagger blade
discovered in Mycenae, for on each side of that
blade is a lion scene. The poet in each poem
shows the same willingness to cling to and to
expand the simile after its purpose has been fulfilled, for example (Γ 2): The noise with which
the Trojans advanced is compared with the cry
of birds, then he adds, ''like the cry of cranes far
ahead in the heavens, which flying from winter and
the heavy storm, move with clangor toward the
streams of the ocean bearing death and destruction to pygmy men, and early in the morning they
begin the baneful struggle.'' Here the pleasure
the poet felt in the cranes leads him away from his
story to a detailed description of the object with
which he illustrated his narrative. Exactly the
same poetic detachment is found in the Odyssey
(τ 205): When the disguised Odysseus calmly
told Penelope that he had seen her husband, ''she
melted to tears like the melting snow, snow on
the top of a lofty mountain, after the west wind
has caused it to fall, and then as it melts the rivers
run full to the sea.'' Here we almost forget Penelope in thinking of the snow, how it came, how
it melts, and how it finds its way to the rivers.
Such similes abound in each poem.

Both poems add to the effectiveness of the
similes by an occasional touch of human interest.
In the Iliad (Θ 559) the poet compares the camp-
fires in the plain of Troy and their beauty to a

night "when in the heaven the stars shine round the clear full moon, when all the air is still, and every cliff and headland towers distinct, and all the stars are seen, and a shepherd rejoices in his heart." It was not enough for the poet to picture this scene of beauty, there must be some one to see it and to rejoice in it, even if that person be only a shepherd. In the Odyssey (χ 302) the poet thus describes Odysseus and those who helped him in the slaughter of the suitors:

And they like unto strong-taloned, hook-beaked vultures when swooping down from the mountains they rush at smaller birds, birds which fly close to the earth in terror, and the vultures darting at them destroy them, for they can neither defend themselves nor escape, and men gaze at the sport with delight.

Finally the comparison of the slow withdrawal of Ajax from superior foes with the slow movements of a sluggish ass which little children are attempting to drive from a field of grain seems to be the conception of the same poet who likened the restlessness of Odysseus to the activity of a sausage which a man constantly whirls and turns over a heavy fire and the sausage is kept from burning solely by the speed with which it is turned. Indeed the similes of the two poems show such a similarity and variety, such a wealth of the powers of observation, and such an ability to seize on the essential and striking features of the objects compared that they could hardly have originated except in the resourceful brain of the same creative genius.

The separatist argument that the bards are more often in evidence in the Odyssey than in the Iliad is easily explained by the fact that in the Odyssey the bards are to be found at the palace of some great king, such as Odysseus, Agamemnon, or Alcinous, but in the Iliad the Greeks are in camp and there is little place or occasion for the presence of the bard. Bards were known to the poet of the Iliad, as is shown by the mention of Thamyris, who lost his sight boasting that he could excel even the Muses in song.

The bards are not introduced into the Odyssey for their own sake or for their songs. They are the means by which the poet solved his greatest and most difficult problem. The story of the Iliad is not complex, therefore the poet is not obliged for the sake of the actors in the poem to repeat what is already known to his own audience; the action of the Iliad has the same audience and the same general background throughout. The story of the Iliad furnishes its own interpretation, but in the Odyssey the case is far different. In that poem three distinct groups of hearers are to be considered: the poet's own audience, the people of Ithaca, and the Phaeacians who were the people of Alcinous. The method by which Homer met this difficulty is one of the greatest proofs of his genius. He wished to repeat little or nothing already known, yet he must keep each of these three groups informed without retelling what was already known to the others. He could

assume that his own audience was acquainted with
the story of the Iliad and the traditions which lay
around it, hence knew of Odysseus; but he could
not assume that an audience in Ithaca had any
clear ideas in regard to the events connected with
the war at Troy; yet he could not repeat for the
sake of the Ithacans a story already known to
his own, the poet's, hearers. This difficulty was
overcome by the creation of the bard and having
him sing a few snatches from Trojan themes, thus
creating the impression that the general outlines
of the tale were already well-known and therefore
need not be repeated. The fact that the bard,
Phemius, was not allowed to sing his song, and
that we have only a brief summary, "and he sang
of the baleful return of the Achaeans, which Pallas
Athena had brought upon them in their departure
from Troy" shows that the bard was not introduced for the sake of his song, but to help out a
bit of poetic mechanism. After we have listened
to these few words from Phemius we know that
the story of Troy is familiar to the poet's own
hearers and to the men of Ithaca, but there still
remains a third audience, the people of Alcinous,
which must also be kept informed. It was necessary, too, that this third audience should be interested in the hero and eager to hear from his own
lips the story of his wandering, for without that
interest his long tale could not be told. Nothing
related in the earlier books has been told to this
audience of the Phaeacians, so that the poet must

start in afresh to win the interest of a new group
of hearers. That not a single device for arousing
the interest either of the poet's own audience or
of the people of Ithaca is repeated before this
third audience is proof of Homer's wonderful
resourcefulness. When the hero came into the
presence of the Phaeacians he at first hid his
identity, since he had no reason to believe that
they had any interest in Odysseus. But when he
showed that wonderful skill in the athletic con-
tests they were interested in him for his own sake,
whoever he might prove to be. The bard then
repeatedly sang a few snatches about the glories
of Odysseus and his exploits at Troy, so that we
know they were interested in Odysseus, wherever
he might be, and the athlete's glory, won by an
unnamed stranger, easily merges into that of the
hero. It was only by withholding the name of
Odysseus, when Arete asked him his name, that
the poet could show to Odysseus how great was
his heroic renown in the land of the Phaeacians,
and it was only by the glory he had won as a
nameless victor that the Phaeacians could accept
without questioning and at once this unknown
stranger as the illustrious Odysseus, whose praises
the bard had just been singing.

No audience not aroused to enthusiasm by
what Odysseus had done and by the songs it had
heard would have listened to the long story of
his wanderings. The real purpose of the games
and the songs was to create this enthusiasm.

Strange as it may seem the starting point for the destructive criticism of the Odyssey carried on by Kirchhoff and all his school lies in the fact that when Arete, the queen of the Phaeacians, asked Odysseus his name, he evaded the answer. Had he replied at once, "I am Odysseus," she might have asked, "Who is Odysseus? I never heard of him before." This would have been an embarrassing position for a great hero. If she had known of the fame of Odysseus, she might have said, "You have no marks of that hero, and I know you are not, since you came here dressed in the clothing I made myself." This would have killed the Odyssey right at the start, yet it is just such poetic absurdity that these great critics demanded of the poet. Homer builded far better. When Odysseus arose to speak and to tell his name, he knew that the story of Troy and his own exploits were well known to his hearers, for twice the bard had sung of them; not much indeed, but just enough to show how familiar they were with Odysseus and with Trojan traditions. He knows, as he rises, the enthusiasm they have for him because of the athletic skill which he has just displayed, he knows their enthusiasm for the heroic Odysseus, and he also knows that their acquaintance with Trojan tales has freed him from the necessity of repeating for their sake a story already known to the poet's own audience. Odysseus can thus begin the narrative of his wanderings with the words, "The wind bearing me from Ilium brought me to the land of the Cicones," and he feels no necessity to make a single reference to the exploits at Troy.

The songs of Demodocus thus served a double purpose: they showed that Odysseus would find an audience eager to listen and, of equal importance, they made it possible for him to take for granted a knowledge of the tale of Troy and permitted him to begin the story of his own wanderings without a hint of what had happened there.

Just before Odysseus left the Phaeacians to start for Ithaca Demodocus sang again, but there is no hint as to the theme of his song. All that the poet tells us is: "And among them sang the divine bard, Demodocus, honored by the people." There was no longer any need to introduce anyone or to relieve the poet from the burden of repeating a familiar tale, hence the unremembered song.

Phemius did a like service in Ithaca. In the first book his brief song of the fate of the Achaeans shows that here the story of Troy needs no retelling. Hence even Odysseus on his return, although he told his wife of his wanderings and adventures, never mentioned the fact that he had been at Troy nor narrated a single event that had happened there. Each bard created by his songs the impression that Trojan tales were already known and the poet was thus saved from the necessity of repeating for the sake of the audiences in the poem a tale already familiar to his own hearers.

The various shrewd devices by which the poet overcame the necessity of repeating familiar tales have convinced me that the Iliad and the Odyssey are not repeating traditions already known, but that they, too, are new and original creations, not old material put into verse, but new material created for new poems. Without an Iliad there would have been but scant tradition in regard to the wrath of Achilles, and without an Odyssey there would have been scant tradition in regard to the return of Odysseus.

No bard is allowed to finish his song, and we are given but a brief indication of the theme, except of the song by Demodocus telling of the love of Ares and Aphrodite. This song was quite apart from heroic traditions and was intended to represent a Phaeacian song, sung at their banquet to delight their leader and his people, as well as their guest, and to give some indication of the things which delighted that pleasure-loving, sensuous people.

The failure to appreciate the fact that the bards were introduced as a poetic device and not for their songs has caused all that immense and futile literature from Welcker to Finsler, which has tried to reconstruct the original poetry of Homer out of such songs as Phemius and Demodocus are supposed to have sung. No necessity for the bards existed in the Iliad, hence they have no part in that poem. No one doubts that bards lived before the Iliad was created, so that the failure of the poet to make use of them must have been from choice and not from ignorance. They were a poetic necessity in the Odyssey, they were not in the Iliad, and their presence or absence is no test of authorship.

There are no tests of language, customs, or civilization which show that the Iliad and the Odyssey were not created in the same age. We must remember that a poet is to be measured by what he says, not by what he omits, and that even what he says is poetry. No one could reconstruct Milton's theology from his poetry, if that poetry were the only source of our knowledge. We should imagine that his gods were much like those of Homer, for each poet begins his poem with an appeal to the Muse. Hamlet might seem to belong to the age when men fought with bows and slings, for he speaks of "The slings and arrows of outrageous fortune," yet Marcellus in that same play asks, "Why such daily cast of brazen cannon?"

In some places Milton's theology seems and is purely pagan, while in other places it is purely Christian; and Shakespeare in the same play refers to slings, arrows, and brazen cannon, each according to his own poetic fancy. Until we can prove that Homer in one passage failed to mention, because he did not know of it, something which he mentioned in some other passage, we cannot establish the existence of various cultural strata in Homeric poetry.

Homeric scholars are heavily in debt to the work of our great archaeologists, whose discoveries have so completely demolished many of the most vaunted proofs of the disintegrators. Not a single discovery made at Troy, Tiryns, Mycenae, or elsewhere has vindicated one of all their many assertions. Without the great finds in the realm of Priam and of Agamemnon it would have been impossible to convince honest doubters of the historical reality of Troy or of the greatness of Mycenae, and to reëstablish the belief that the Trojan War was something more than fancy. Had Schliemann accepted the universally triumphant beliefs of his day and doubted the unity and reliability of the Iliad, Troy might never have been discovered, and lovers of Homer could hardly have dared to believe in Homeric unity.

The archaeologists, men who deal with tangible objects, are as a rule Homeric unitarians. It is a great pleasure to quote the words of Wace, whose high standing is guaranteed by the fact that he has been for several years and still is the director of the British School of Archaeology at Athens. He wrote in a recent number of the *Edinburgh Review* (July, 1919) as follows:

The Wolfian cloud still hangs over the study of Homer. It has had a blighting effect on Homeric study which otherwise, thanks to the advance of Archaeology, might have made surprising progress. . . . . We must abandon the Wolfian theory and all it entails. The Iliad and the Odyssey were written down when composed, and the text has not been substantially altered since. The longer we devote ourselves to the actual poems, the more shall we be refreshed, and the more will the faith in our creed be strengthened.

This complete change of attitude on the part of unprejudiced investigators is due to the fact that a few years ago scholars wearied of their efforts to build a worthy structure out of the assumptions of the higher critics and in their weariness turned once more to the study of Homer.

CHAPTER V

THE CONTRADICTIONS

Some of the arguments against Homeric unity already mentioned have been advanced by one group of critics, others by others; but there is one argument upon which all are agreed. They all agree that there are, in both poems, certain inconsistencies and contradictions, and that these are of such a nature as to make unity of plan and unity of authorship impossible.

Inconsistencies like the following are cited: When Athena, in the guise of Mentor, and Telemachus come to Pylos, they find a great gathering of the people assembled for a sacrifice. Soon, however, the people are forgotten, and what was a multitude becomes a little family group. Later when these same two travelers arrive at Sparta on the occasion of a great wedding feast, they find the palace so crowded that it seems impossible for others to be received. The wedding in turn is soon ignored and is replaced by a small domestic circle, where Helen is busy with her household cares. When it is time for the guests to retire, the bride, the groom, the entertainers, are all forgotten. Telemachus declines an invitation to make a short visit, and yet tarries at least a

month, with no explanation for the delay. The
Greeks before Troy at one time are protected by
a moat and a wall; at another, both defenses are
ignored. Patroclus tells Nestor that he is in a
great hurry and may not be seated, that Achilles
is impatient, and, now that he has the information
for which he came, he must return with speed to
Achilles; yet he does not return until after action
which fills four books. Even then he forgets his
errand and his message. After Diomede has
wounded both Aphrodite and Ares, he shrinks
from facing Glaucus, lest he prove to be a god,
saying, "I would not fight with a god." Hector,
after he has been for the most part a hero in flight,
challenges the best of the Greeks to meet him in
single combat. All seem afraid, yet they dare
not refuse; and, oddly enough, no one refers to
the duel fought on that very day by Paris and
Menelaus, a duel which had proved a fiasco and
the terms of which had been treacherously broken.

These examples might be indefinitely extended.
Nothing in Homeric criticism has been so simple,
so easy as this. No scholar who has set out to
gather Homeric inconsistencies has ever returned
empty-handed, and when once a critic has acquired
a taste for this sort of thing he soon convinces
himself that Homer has little else than contradictions. All these are freely admitted, they are
many, they are found throughout the Iliad and
the Odyssey, and they cannot be removed without
destroying the best of both poems.

Fifty years ago most believers in Homeric unity defended that belief by the assumption that all these contradictions had been added to the poems by interpolators. They believed that by removing these suspected passages harmony and unity might be restored, an assumption that has led to the rejection of practically every verse in Homer. No one has ever given a satisfying explanation of the origin of these interpolations, or of their acceptance by bards and public. It may be easy to suppose that some prosaic and dull bard removed good verses and substituted inferior ones, but here the supposition ends. For there still remains the harder necessity of getting other bards to accept this change, and, harder still, the necessity of getting an intelligent audience, already familiar with the better text, to accept this inferior poetry.

This explanation, on the basis of the interpolation of inferior scenes, demands not only one inferior bard, but an inferior audience, and a like inferiority in all other bards. The creator of nonsense verses might have pride in his own production and not recognize his own stupidity. But how could he get his inferior version accepted?

The contradiction is not removed by assuming a second poet, for that second poet would be most careful not to betray himself by any slips. The whole scheme of higher criticism involves the existence of a group of poets determined to give up their own individuality and to merge their own

work into that of another. They have so completely mastered his language, his meter, his
style, that their work cannot be detected. Yet
they were so ignorant of the very writings they
imitated and into which they were eager to merge
their own efforts that they made, unconsciously,
these contradictions. Certainly the imitator would
above everything strive not to betray himself by
inconsistencies. But to the original genius, the
creator, such things would be of no moment; he
has nothing to conceal and he need never fear that
a slip may betray him. Even counterfeiters are
detected by the very consistency with which they
follow the writing of the names they forge. A
recent expert has said that no man ever writes
his own signature twice in exactly the same way,
while the counterfeiter exactly repeats the signature he is imitating.[1] These inconsistencies in
Homer are proof that they come from an original
genius, from one who is himself, and not from
one who is following the style of another or who
is interpolating his own into another's poetry.
All these contradictions or shifts of poetic purpose
may be explained on the theory of one creative
genius, but are impossible of explanation on the
assumption that different parts were added by
servile imitators or followers.

Homeric contradictions may be divided into
three groups: actual contradictions, due to the
lapse in the memory of the poet, those in which no

[1] Arthur S. Chapman, *American Magazine*, May, 1920.

poetic plan or purpose can be detected; assumed contradictions, due solely to the failure of the critics properly to translate or to understand the simple meaning of the poet; and finally, inconsistencies arising from the manner in which the poems were presented, that is, from a changed poetic purpose, or from the shifting point of view of the various actors in the poems.

Actual contradictions in Homer are very few and these few of trifling importance. The list given by Mahaffy contains but one actual contradiction, and that one is grossly misstated.[2] "The fact that the same heroes are killed two or three times over may pass as unimportant." As a matter of fact not a single hero or person is slain twice or dies twice in Homer. The only slip of this sort in all Homer is found in the fact that Pylaemenes, a king of the Paphlagonians, was slain in E 576, and subsequently mourns the death of his son (N 658). Pylaemenes was purely a characterless figure in the Iliad, who took no part in the action and was introduced only to be slain. The poet, evidently forgetting that he had introduced such a person and had had him killed, in a later book mentions the death of a son of Pylaemenes and the mourning of the father. This petty ruler was of no importance in the poem alive or dead, so that it takes rather careful study to notice that the king who mourns had been slain eight books previously. This, as I have already

[2] *History of Greek Literature*, I, 83.

said, is the only contradiction of the sort in either poem.

A certain Schedius, the son of Perimedes, was slain, as was another Schedius, the son of Iphitus. The fact that the name of the father was given in each case shows that there was no confusion. It was no easy matter for even a Greek to make a new name for each minor actor. Homer used the same name over and over, except for the leading actors; with the leading actors identity of name would have caused confusion. There were four Trojans and one Greek with the name Chromius, one Greek and two Trojans with the name Melanippus, and one Greek and two Trojans had the name Adrastus. There can be no doubt that the poet intended two persons by the name of Schedius, one the son of Iphitus, the other the son of Perimedes, so that the statement made by Mahaffy that "the same heroes are killed two or three times over" is an error.

The contradiction in regard to Pylaemenes, who was killed in the fifth book and mourns his son in the thirteenth, is a real contradiction. But no part of the plot depended on Pylaemenes; neither his death nor his grief has any bearing on the story. No one could assume that the bards who committed the poems to memory failed to notice that the Pylaemenes who mourned the loss of a son had himself been slain a few books previously. The very fact that this contradiction was never removed is the best possible proof of the fidelity with which the Homeric text had been preserved. We may confidently assume that bards who could not or would not rectify this manifest error had neither the power nor the inclination to change the Homeric tradition.

Such errors as the above abound in literatures where the author had the advantage of printing, proof reading, and all the modern methods for detecting mistakes. In the first edition of Thackeray's *Newcomes* one of the prominent characters dies, comes back to life, and calmly continues to act until the end of the story. Lowell ranks *Don Quixote* as one of the greatest achievements of the world's literature. This work was printed and given to the public by the author himself, yet it contains such glaring contradictions that it seems impossible that they could have escaped the notice of the printer. The contradiction in regard to Pylaemenes comes long after his death, so that one could hardly notice it, and Pylaemenes is too unimportant to give any weight to the contradiction. In *Don Quixote,* on the other hand, the contradictions are so open that the reader turns back only a page or two in order to make sure that he has not misread the text. The four leading actors in this great work of Cervantes are Don Quixote, his horse Rozinante, Sancho, and the ass. In chapter twenty-three Sancho's ass was stolen, to his infinite misery. Then the squire urged that they proceed, whereupon "the knight led the way and Sancho followed his master sitting sideways on his ass." While thus sitting, Sancho complained, "The theft of my ass makes me but a sorry traveler on foot." Cervantes, in Part Two of his great work, poked fun at himself for this contradiction, but he did not think it worth while to rewrite the scene. Again, Sancho's wife was, in one place, Maria, in another, Teresa.

The literary canon that contradictions make unity of authorship impossible, a canon which was deified at the middle of the last century, is at such absolute variance with well-known facts that one can only wonder at the literary blindness which created it or accepted it. This canon is thus stated by Mahaffy:[3] "Wherever there is a plain violation of logical consistency, we have not the work of a single poet telling his own story." *Don Quixote* suffices to show the futility of this rule. We must remember also that *Don Quixote* was not the work of a young and untried genius, but of a man nearing old age, who had tried many fields of literature and who had produced many great dramas. These contradictions, therefore, were not due to inexperience. Even an artist of the delicate workmanship of Vergil, in a single book of the Aeneid,[4] described the wooden horse in one passage as made of fir, in another as made of maple, and in another as made of oak.

Wood, writing in 1769, twenty-six years before Wolf's *Prolegomena* appeared, said:

[3] *Loc. cit.*
[4] II, 16, 112, 186.

Cassandra had laid open to Anchises the destination of his family for Italy. It is pointed out to Aeneas in various manners, but most explicitly by the ghost of Creüsa, who not only informs him that he is to go to Italy, but describes the part of it where he is to reign. Yet in a few lines we see the Trojans embark, without knowing where to go. Should we proceed to examine the whole action of the Aeneid in this manner, we might observe little inaccuracies of the same kind, which are not to be found so frequently in Homer.[5]

This evidence is of the greater weight from the fact that it comes from a competent observer at a time when there was no Homeric Question. He was trying to prove nothing, simply stating his own observation that contradictions are not so frequent in Homer as in Vergil. Such contradictions abound in literary masterpieces of undoubted unity. In my opinion they are proof of just the opposite of that which the critics assume, that is, they show that the creative genius has his mind and his eye fixed on the general plan, the leading idea, while the imitator could not see this; he would notice the details, the workmanship.

The second class of contradictions consists of those which result from the failure of the critics to translate or to understand the simple meaning of the poet. This class is almost unlimited in number and is a sad commentary on the ruthless manner in which Homer has been mutilated and ignored. The few following illustrations from the writings of the most famous scholars will suffice: Bergk began his *Griechische Literaturgeschichte*

[5] *Op. cit.,* p. 20.

on a mammoth scale, devoting over one thousand
pages to the early epic. This volume he lived to
see published; and as it was written by one of the
most illustrious of Greek scholars, it should be
the ideal of a literary history. Bergk, although
a defender of Homeric unity, regarded entire
scenes and books as interpolations and ruthlessly
removed them. The contradictions furnished him
his criteria for making most of his decisions. The
following example may be selected as one on which
he laid great stress: Amphinomus, one of the most
kindly and gentle of the suitors, treated the beggar Odysseus with such tender consideration that
Odysseus tried to warn him of his impending
danger. But the warning was not heeded; he
remained with the suitors and was slain. The
poet tells us in advance that Amphinomus was
not to escape the doom which Athena had prepared for him, for she had decreed that he was to
die at the hands of Telemachus. Bergk found a
great contradiction here and wrote: "Later, when
the suitors are slain, Amphinomus does not
appear, a proof either of a poetic error or that
the description of the death of the suitors has
been changed in transmission." One wonders
that when Bergk wrote this sentence he did not
have sufficient curiosity to re-read the Homeric
account of the slaughter of the suitors. If he
had done so, he would have found eight verses
wholly given to the description of the death of
this very Amphinomus at the hands of Tele-

machus. These eight verses are in every standard edition of the Odyssey; if Bergk had a copy of the Odyssey, they were in that copy.

Bethe, because of an assumed contradiction, rejects as an interpolation the episode (A 194 ff.) in which the goddess Athena stops the attempt of Achilles to assault or murder the king:[6] "It would be a tame climax for Achilles to throw his scepter to the ground after he had already flashed a sword in the face of the Greeks"; and again: "The throwing down of the scepter appears as a cheap anticlimax, since the sword has already flown from the scabbard." Yet the Greek to which he refers is the simplest that could be written; the verb is in the imperfect tense and can be translated only, "While he was drawing the sword from its sheath." When Athena came she said to him, "Draw not thy sword." She did not command him to return it to the scabbard, for the good reason that it had not yet been drawn. There is no anticlimax and no contradiction in Homer's account. Bethe's assumptions and the ponderous book he wrote rest on a mistaken translation of a perfectly simple and a remarkably unambiguous sentence.

Mahaffy selects as especially notable the following contradiction:[7]

In the races of the twenty-third book Diomede contends with the horses he took from Aeneas in the fifth book, and no mention is made of the much finer horses

[6] *Homer: Dichtung und Sage*, 188.
[7] *History of Greek Literature*, I, 83.

he carried off in the tenth book. Some allusion to them here was not only natural, but necessary, if a single poet had been thinking out the story.

The great superiority of the horses of Rhesus over those taken from Aeneas is a pure and unfounded assumption. We know nothing about the horses of Rhesus except the words of the craven spy, Dolon, who hoped so to arouse the eagerness of Diomede and Odysseus for these horses that they would save him. He told them that he had never seen nobler or more beautiful steeds, that they were as white as snow and as swift as the wind. Nestor, when he saw them coming at night, compared them to the rays of the sun, evidently a reference to their color. But it is to be noted that the real expert in horseflesh, Diomede, did not pass any judgment upon them. When Aeneas drove his steeds to battle and Diomede saw them, he knew all about them, had their virtues and their pedigree on the tip of his tongue, and said to his squire (E 265): "Those horses are of the stock which Zeus gave to Tros in return for Ganymede, the very finest breed on which the sun shines. If we can get that team, we shall win great glory." This is the opinion of a real expert. The statement that the horses of Rhesus were superior to those taken from Aeneas ignores both their divine stock and the enthusiastic appraisal of the calm and competent Diomede.

Wilamowitz' great contradiction in regard to the seasons of the Odyssey, based on the position of the stars, was the result of his own ignorance in astronomy, and was a mistake which the merest novice in that science could easily have rectified.

The next contradiction which I shall cite may well seem to have reached the bottom of absurdity. When Odysseus set foot on the land of the Phaeacians, he had long been tossed on the sea, was without clothing, was famished, miserable, and wretched. While in this plight, he heard the laughing voices of Nausicaa and her companions at play. Breaking off the branches of a tree to cover his nakedness, he started to meet her that he might beg her for food, for clothing, and for guidance. His appearance must have been most repulsive, yet, by means of words of clever and enticing flattery, he overcame this difficulty and won her respect:

I beg thee, lady, tell me if thou art a goddess, or a mortal. If a goddess, then I liken thee to Artemis, the daughter of Zeus, for such is thy stature and thy bearing; but if thou art mortal, then thrice blessed thy father, thrice blessed thy mother, thrice blessed thy brothers. Surely their hearts must swell within them in glad pride because of thee.[7]

Here the poetic soul of Fick detected a great contradiction and he cried out, "How did Odysseus know that this fair maiden had any brothers?" *Odysseus konnte gar nicht wissen, ob Brüder vorhanden waren. (Entstehung der Odyssee, p. 181.)*

This might seem to be the bottom in critical absurdity, but that honor seems to fall to the

7 ʒ 149.

long list of editors who have repeated the evidence
for contradictions in the simile of the wasps found
in Π 265 ff. This simile paints the fury with
which the impatient followers of Achilles, under
the command of Patroclus, rushed to battle:

> They rushed forth like wasps which have a nest by
> the side of a road, wasps which little boys constantly
> anger by always stirring them up, the young rascals,
> and thus they get many into trouble; for if any unsus-
> pecting traveler goes quietly along and disturbs them,
> they all rush out with fury and try to drive him away
> from their nest. With spirit like to theirs the Myrmidons
> moved on.

This scene, which forms the basis of the simile,
has been repeated a million times. Few country
lads, indeed, can say that they never threw a stone
or a club into a nest of wasps and then concealed
themselves to watch the attack the angry wasps
made upon some innocent wayfarer. It is a
familiar fact that wasps will not fight or sting
unless aroused in some such way as Homer
describes. The *New International Encyclopaedia*
says under the word "wasps": "Wasps are not
dangerous except when disturbed. When they
are flying about they are harmless unless irri-
tated." This Homeric simile is so simple, so true
to life, and it deals with such a well-known matter,
that it is difficult to grasp the reasons why so
many editors have failed to comprehend it. Fried-
länder argued that we have here a double version
and a contradiction. "In the first version the
wasps were roused by the children; in the second,

by the traveler." Of course the only reason the
wasps rush at that innocent traveler is because
the naughty boys have already stirred them up.
Nitzsch accepts the theory of the double version,
but rejects the rousing of the wasps by either the
children or the traveler. He thinks the simile
would gain force if the attack of the wasps is conceived as unprovoked, and would reduce the whole
simile and its contents to the simple but vigorous
statement: "The Myrmidons rushed to battle with
all the fury of undisturbed wasps." Wilamowitz
accepts this nonsense in his *Die Ilias und Homer*
(p. 127). What is most surprising in this is the
fact that it is quoted by Doctor Leaf, with evident
approval, in his note to Π 259. Just as Doctor
Leaf gave up his doubts about the geography
of the Iliad when he got away from the critics,
so, I am sure, he will laugh to think that he ever
quoted this absurdity, "The simile would gain
force, if the wasps' attack is conceived as unprovoked," if he ever takes the trouble to walk by
and to observe a quiet nest of unprovoked wasps.

The first class of contradictions was due to
the nods of the poet, the second to the nods of
the critics. The third class of contradictions or
inconsistencies is due to the manner in which the
poetry was presented. Most of these contradictions fall into a category which has been named
"Devices of temporary expediency." This idea
goes back, in a measure, to Aristarchus, but the
rediscovery and scientific application of this prin-

ciple to modern Homeric criticism has been one
of the chief reasons for the reëstablishment of the
belief in the unity of Homer. It was first worthily
employed by Dr. Carl Rothe, in a little pamphlet
of thirty-six pages, *Die Bedeutung der Wider-
sprüche für die Homerische Frage* (Berlin, 1891).

The scientific value and aesthetic worth of
German scholarship has, no doubt, been greatly
discredited by the advocates of higher criticism,
especially from the fact that it was in Germany
that this theory received its so-called scientific
birth and most of its support. Wolf, Lachmann,
Kirchhoff, Wilamowitz, and a long list of famous
names have done much to convince the world that
German erudition is blind and stupid, bent on
making false facts in order to support a false
theory. But Goethe and Schiller regained or
retained their honest vision and vindicated the
poetic unity of Homer; Schliemann spurned the
arguments of the critics and found both Troy, the
city of Priam, and Mycenae, the home of Agamemnon, and Dörpfeld later gave to these discoveries
their scientific and lasting interpretation; Ludwich has kept the text of Homer free from those
linguistic vagaries which threatened to substitute
conjectural for traditional texts; Rothe set on
foot the ideas in regard to contradictions which
must prevail; and Stürmer and Drerup have written and are now writing the most detailed and
elaborate defense of Homeric unity with which I
am familiar, a defense which covers practically

every verse of both poems, including even the parts most suspected. When we balance the ledger and figure both the debit and the credit accounts, we must honestly admit that the world of Homeric scholarship is overwhelmingly in debt to Germany.

Doctor Rothe's great contribution to Homeric study consists in the evidence that this poetry is not complicated and involved, but simple and carried by a single thread, each scene being constructed or planned for its own sake. For example, the poet wished to give a picture of private and domestic life, and with this in view he planned the parting scene between Hector and Andromache. No other actor than Hector could be used. The poet therefore had him leave the field at just that moment when he was most urgently needed as a fighter, ostensibly for the purpose of urging that sacrifices be offered to Athena. This was a service the lowliest soldier could have performed. But the lowliest soldier could not play a part in the scene with Andromache, and so Hector was spared from the battle. Each scene in Homer must have the attention of the audience as it is heard. It is not enough that the hearer was interested yesterday, and that there will be another scene to interest him to-morrow. The poet must focus his own and his hearers' attention on the scene that is now being recited. The poet has always a definite notion of his actors, for they are consistent throughout.

But he takes little interest in the way in which he poses them or brings them on or sends them off the stage.

The epic poet had no means but language for denoting the coming or going of actors or for a change in scenery or background. Often a person appears, acts, then disappears, without a word from the poet to tell us he is gone. Had the poet described the coming or going of each participant in the action, the narrative would be dull and tedious. Much is left to the intelligence and imagination of his hearers. Gods and heroes slip from place to place with amazing suddenness and in absolute silence. The eye gives the needed information in the theater or in a moving picture, but no such help was at hand for the epic poet. In Φ 17 Achilles laid down his spear; fifty verses later it is back in his hand. The fact that he has it later is proof enough that he must have picked it up, an action we could have seen on the stage, but which must be tacitly assumed in Homer. When Poseidon came over the sea to the battle-field he came in his magnificent chariot drawn by fleet steeds with manes of gold. He shackled them with golden shackles that they should await his return.[8] But when he left the field there is no mention either of his shackled horses or of the method of his going.[9] Zeus had been watching the battle from Mt. Ida,[10] yet all at once he is back in Olympus.[11] Ares was sitting on the outskirts of

[8] N 23.   [10] O 152.
[9] O 219.   [11] Π 431.

the battle with his horses and chariot,[12] but when he arrived, he came apparently on foot.[13] Athena and Hera came to the plain of Troy in a chariot. They unhitched their horses, turned them out to graze, and started to aid the Greeks.[14] But the goddesses apparently forgot their horses and left them there, for their return from the field of battle is told in a single verse: "Athena with Hera returned to Olympus."[15] These apparent slips are all to be explained by the fact that epic poetry depended solely on the ear; if every detail had been given, the poem would have been so encumbered as to be intolerable.

The length of the Iliad, over 15,000 verses, made it impossible for more than a small portion to be recited at a single time. The poet must therefore so plan his work as to assist the bard by making it possible for him to recite at a single time, portions fairly complete, yet so related with what has gone before and with what is yet to be as to create pleasure by recalling what has been already heard and by anticipating that which is to follow. The present division of each poem into twenty-four books is purely arbitrary—so arbitrary, indeed, that a sentence begun in Odyssey β is concluded in the following book. The division was made by the grammarians of Alexandria in order to facilitate references and was based on the twenty-four letters of the Greek alphabet.

[12] E 356. [14] E 775.
[13] E 35. [15] E 907.

Professor Drerup, by means of repeated tests, has found that a skilled reciter can pronounce, with proper intonations, about five hundred Homeric verses per hour, and that the powers of a reciter are practically exhausted in two hours; hence a rhapsodist would be limited on a single occasion to about one thousand verses. With this limit in mind, he started to read the Iliad, and found to his great delight that the poem easily divided itself into such groups, each group, like the whole, having a beginning, a middle, and an end; each complete in itself, yet each a part of the greater unity of the whole.[16] If Homer is read with these two facts in mind, first, that the poems were created to be recited in portions of about one thousand verses each, and, second, that the bard must, without the help of stage setting or background, concentrate the attention on the scene he is then presenting, most of the so-called inconsistencies and contradictions will disappear.

I shall apply these principles to two of the most criticised contradictions in Homer: first, the refusal of Diomede to meet Glaucus, lest he should prove to be a god, despite the fact that he has on that very day wounded both Aphrodite and Ares; and, second, that it was noon twice, apparently, on the same day. In E 127 Athena took the mist from the eyes of Diomede so that he could recognize the gods and thus know and wound Aphrodite. This purpose was realized in verse 330. Diomede perceived the goddess and thrust her with his

16 Drerup, *Das fünfte Buch der Ilias*, 421.

spear. A few verses further on Diomede is described as rushing at Aeneas, although he knew that Apollo protected him, thus clearly showing that the power of miraculous sight still remained with him. Again in verse 815 he recognized Athena at once. The command to wound only Aphrodite was later enlarged by Athena herself and made to include the wounding of Ares. From the time when Athena gave this power to Diomede, in E 127, to the end of that book, he retained this miraculous vision, so that he was able to see and to know the gods. At the end of book five there is plainly a pause in the poem, the field is deserted by the gods, who return to Olympus, and the bard, as well as the hearers, takes a needed rest. No one can read the Iliad without feeling that the poet planned an intermission at this place.

With book six the poem takes a new start. The gift of Athena was a special gift for a special purpose, and both the gift and its purpose were a part of the preceding book. No unprejudiced reader would argue that the gift of miraculous sight was a perpetual gift. It must also be observed that each deity wounded in book five was wounded by the express orders of Athena. When book six opens, Athena has withdrawn from the scene of action, and Diomede has returned to his normal vision and also to his natural fear of fighting one of the gods. When Glaucus appeared, therefore, Diomede, still evidently under the spell

and the excitement of his previous exploits, hesitated to meet him, lest he should prove to be a
god. These words of Diomede would have con-
stituted an impossible contradiction had they
appeared in the previous book, but in book six
Athena and her divine gift are both alike withdrawn, and Diomede is once more a mortal hero
with neither the power to discern nor the will to
fight a divine being.

In Λ 84 occur the words, "As long as it was
morning and the sacred day waxed." This would
seem to indicate the end of the morning, a time
near noon. The battle then beginning continued
through long stretches of intense and apparently
protracted fighting. Then we are suddenly told,
five books later (Π 775), "As long as the sun
bestrode the center of the heaven." The actual
time marked between the end of the morning and
the beginning of the afternoon could hardly be
more than five hours, yet the fighting which has
been pictured as falling in that interval seems
almost endless. The manner of Homeric recitation made it impossible for the poet to picture
events as taking place simultaneously, so that he
never leaves one scene and moves to another by
saying, "While these things were done here, such
other things happened there." He always seems
to say, "After these things were done here, those
things were done there."

At the opening of the Odyssey the poet tells
how the gods planned to send Hermes to the

island of Calypso in order that he might deliver
to her the divine decree to send Odysseus on his
way to Ithaca. As soon as the gods had made
this decision, Athena herself hurried to Ithaca to
set affairs there in order, to encourage Telemachus, and to prepare for the return of Odysseus. This visit of Athena and its consequences
fill about four books and we almost lose sight of
the results of the deliberation of the gods with
which the poem began. At the beginning of the
fifth book the poet had his choice of picturing
Hermes as going to Calypso while Athena was at
Ithaca, or of starting his poem all over again.
The second method was the one the poet chose.
The gods were again assembled, and Hermes was
again ordered to bear to Calypso the unerring
command of the gods. A like problem confronted
the poet who described the long series of battles
which followed on the day after the fruitless
efforts of the embassy to induce Achilles to abandon his wrath. He had the choice of prolonging
the day or of dividing the battles with the exploits
of another night. He had already pictured a night
with crowded events, an assembly, an embassy to
Achilles, and the exploits of Diomede and Odysseus, so that he would hardly care to fill a second
night with kindred or rival incidents, hence prolonged the day and crowded a mass of action
between late morning and early afternoon. The
verses describing this day's fighting number
about five thousand, or almost one third of the

entire Iliad, so that the bard could hardly have
recited it in fewer than five separate appearances. This fact would make it most difficult for
the hearers to notice that all these events belonged
to the same day, or that too much had been
crowded into the few hours of midday. The
multitude of events assigned to this one day is
a part of that poetic economy which chose to
lengthen the day rather than to prolong the poem
by creating and describing the events of another
night on the battle-field under exactly the same
conditions as obtained on the night before.

Many things in Homer are done for a poetic
purpose and when that poetic purpose is once
achieved, the matter itself is forgotten. In book
four the poet desired some act of treachery by
which the oaths should be broken and the Trojans
made to bear the blame, hence the shooting of
Menelaus by Pandarus. This act was not intended
to hurt Menelaus, except in so far as some such
an act was necessary to break the truce and put
the Trojans in the light of perjurers. This purpose was gained by the mere fact of the wound,
so that as soon as the battle was started, a battle
due to this treachery, the wound had no further
poetic purpose and Menelaus became entirely well.
He even offered to accept the challenge which
Hector had made to the best of the Greeks to
engage in a single combat, and that, too, without
a thought of the wound he had received but a few
hours before. In book eleven the great warriors,

Agamemnon, Diomede, and Odysseus, were all so seriously wounded that they were forced to retire from action. They were wounded for this very purpose, that they should retire and thus make it possible for Hector to strike terror into the hearts of the Greeks, to draw Patroclus into the struggle, and by his death to give Achilles a fitting occasion for abandoning his wrath and returning to the combat.

These men were wounded for a temporary poetic purpose, and when that purpose had been gained they came back fully recovered. Diomede, although he had been shot through the foot, was able in but three days to take two prizes in the games. Odysseus, even though he had been so badly wounded in the side that his ribs were exposed, yet competed in the wrestling match, the worst possible thing for sore ribs; and he won the foot race, defeating even the swift-footed Antilochus. The wound of Menelaus lasted only long enough to effect the breaking of the truce and to convict the Trojans of treachery; and the other three nursed their wounds until Achilles came back into action. With the breaking of the truce, Menelaus completely recovered; with the return of Achilles, the wounds of Agamemnon, Diomede, and Odysseus were immediately healed. A second reason for the wounding of these heroes is that it would be a balm to Greek pride to know that Hector could accomplish little so long as these men remained on the field.

Many contradictions depend upon the changed attitude or state of mind of the speaker. Achilles in book nine rejected with dignified anger the appeal of the ambassadors, telling them how dear Briseis was to him, how much he loved her. In this scene Achilles imagined that his great anger because of the insult offered him by Agamemnon was due to his passion for Briseis; but when later, because of the death of Patroclus, his anger had been turned to remorse, he exclaimed: "If only Artemis had slain her on the very day I captured her city" (T 59). The first speech was that of a man in anger; the second the speech of that same man in remorse because of the results of that anger. If the second passage stood without the first, half of its effect would be lost. Again in the same book Achilles told the ambassadors that Hector never dared leave the walls of Troy while he himself was fighting, yet Agamemnon had tried to dissuade Menelaus from meeting Hector in single combat on the ground that even Achilles hesitated to meet Hector in battle. The words used by Achilles in the passage quoted were spoken in disparagement of the Greeks. The exaggerated praise of Hector in the mouth of Agamemnon was intended to discourage and frighten Menelaus.

Finally there are contradictions which may be termed temporal contradictions, such as the fact that in the tenth year of the war Helen points out to Priam the leaders of the Greeks, and he

does not know them or their names; also that a
wall to protect the camp is not built until so late
in the war; and, lastly, the arrival of so many
Trojan allies after the war has already continued
for more than nine years.

We may assume the following background for
the war of the Iliad:[17] The Greeks, in large numbers and well-prepared, came to attack Troy. The
Trojans, protected by the strong walls of their
citadel, refused to meet the foe in the open field,
and contented themselves with occasional sallies
on the camp or against scattered divisions of the
enemy. Their plan was much like that of Pericles
in the early years of the Peloponnesian War.
Supplies came regularly into the beleaguered
city, and the Greeks seemed unable to capture
it by storm or to reduce it by starvation. After
several years of this vain effort the Greeks
realized that Troy could not be taken so long as
she kept her communications in the rear open,
and they determined to cut them. This resulted
in the "Great Foray," in which Briseis and
Chryseis became spoils of war. The Greeks
were already in control of the sea and now that
they were able to intercept or threaten supplies
coming by land, Troy must fight or fall, and thus
for the first time she called upon her allies.
Since the ability to withstand a siege when protected by such impregnable walls as those of Troy
depended on the presence of supplies, it was to

17 This is based largely on Leaf's *Troy*.

the interest of the invested city to have as few
as possible to feed. Had she summoned her allies
while she was still pursuing the defensive policy,
she would have hastened her own ruin and would
have brought upon herself the very calamity
Lysander brought upon Athens after the victory
at Aegospotami.

But this defensive policy had to be abandoned
when once they were cut off from the source of
supplies and they must summon reinforcements.
This explains why Rhesus and so many others
had just arrived or were arriving to assist the
Trojans during the action of the Iliad. The
exhausted resources of the Trojans and the re-
sulting presence of their allies caused a complete
change in the plans of the war, for the Greeks were
no longer the attacking army but the attacked.
The real cause of this change was the success of
the Greek efforts in forcing the Trojans into
starvation, but the poet hides the true reason
under the poetic device of the ''Wrath.'' This
was put at just the time when the economic dis-
tress forced the Trojans to assume the aggressive.
With this change of policy the Greeks must prepare, not for attack, but for defense, hence the
necessity for building the wall and digging the
great ditch. The wall would have been of little
use during the earlier years of the war, but now,
with the Trojans desperate and reinforced by
their allies, and all determined to fight, the camp
of the Greeks must be protected.

It was the unexpected prowess of the Trojans, but above all the sudden presence of the allies, that crushed the spirit of Agamemnon. After the siege had been pressed for ten years he found the Trojans suddenly strengthened. This unanticipated accession of allied forces explains his words of disappointment (B 130) : "But allies from many cities are here, who baffle me greatly and thwart my efforts to sack the well-walled city Troy." Just when he thought the siege had ruined the power of the enemy and that the Trojans were his only antagonists he found that his hopes were baffled by the arrival of the allies. Immediately the whole aspect of things was changed; the Greeks who had been thinking only of the ruin of the Trojans were forced to provide for their own safety, a wall was built, pickets were posted, spies sent out, and military tactics were adopted, as if it were indeed the beginning of the war. Many events, such as the muster of the troops, the report of the Trojan picket on the numbers of the Greeks, the duel between Paris and Menelaus, the view from the walls, do not strictly belong to the tenth year of the war; but the poet must give some impression of the appearance of the army and of the tactics employed, of the regal bearing of Agamemnon, of the beauty of Helen, and of her mental attitude toward her present and her former husband. Since he did not describe the earlier years of the war the poet must insert them in the only part he did describe.

Homer's plan of crowding all the events of the poem into the space of a few days did not permit him to picture both ends of a long war, hence scenes are put into the last few days which in a prose narrative would have come much earlier.[18]

Shakespeare, in the advice given by Polonius to his son, Laertes, furnishes a perfect parallel to these inconsistencies. That young man had long been in France, whence he returned to Denmark that he might be present at the coronation. Yet, when he was on the point of going back, his father told him how to dress in France, and added many details of conduct, as if he were leaving Denmark for the first time. No doubt this scene from Hamlet would have better suited the first home-leaving of Laertes, but as that fell outside the limits of the poem the poet must either insert it here or omit it altogether.

It was on the basis of such contradictions as have been given that Lachmann and all his followers erected the theory that Homer originally consisted of a mass of small songs which a learned commission later grouped around a central theme, and this commission could not or would not reshape these songs so as to remove the contradictions. There are two proofs, among many, which seem to me to make the idea that Homer originated by the collection of independent songs impossible: first, the manner in which the different actors are introduced, and, second, the description

[18] "Assumed Duration of the War of the Iliad," *Class. Phil.*, VIII, 445.

of the different persons whose forms the various gods assume.

Homer has two methods of introducing his actors: first, he gives a fairly detailed introduction at the time of their first appearance, or, second, an actor appears with no introduction but his name, then disappears, to be given later a detailed introduction just before he begins to play an important part in the action of the poem. When Nestor first appeared he was introduced thus:

Then Nestor the sweet-voiced arose, the eloquent orator of the men of Pylos, from whose lips speech sweeter than honey flowed. Two generations of men had come and gone since he was born, and now he was ruling over the third.

This lengthy description shows that he is to have a prominent part in the poem. He is formally introduced nowhere else, so that when he appears in any other part of Homer it is always as a leader who is perfectly well-known. When Briseis first moves across the stage she is only a mute figure, hence there is no detailed introduction, but as she leaves the scene we are confident that she will reappear and we shall learn more about her. When she comes on again (T 287), we learn that she is a widow whose husband fell at the hands of Achilles, who also slew her three brothers and destroyed her city at the time he slew her husband. In a similar manner Patroclus comes on the stage and walks away in silence, and with no introduction, but he, too, will reappear and be introduced (Λ 770) be-

fore he takes a prominent part in the poem. The
first book was so crowded with excitement that
Briseis and Patroclus remained mute and waited
for a lull in the action, and waited also to be introduced until they were to take a prominent place
on the center of the stage.

Exactly similar is the method of the Odyssey.
When Eurycleia comes on, we are told her name,
the name of her father, and of her father's father,
how she came into the family of Odysseus, and
what price had been paid for her. This detailed
introduction points to the prominent part she is
to take in the later events of the poem. She is
introduced thus only here; in the subsequent
books she comes and goes as one perfectly well-
known to the hearers. The method of her introduction is similar to that by which Nestor was
brought before the hearers of the Iliad. In the
earlier poem Briseis and Patroclus came on as
mutes to be introduced in later books. So the
first reference to the swineherd is in a chance
remark that "The suitors supposed that Telemachus was out in the fields with the flocks, or
perhaps he might be with the swineherd."[19] The
poet gives no inkling of who the swineherd is
when he is mentioned for the first time, since he
is not to act for several days, but before he begins
to take a prominent part we are told the story
of his life and how it happens that so fine a spirit
should be found in a bondsman.[20]

[19] δ 640. [20] o 403.

Had the formal and detailed introduction of Nestor, Patroclus, Eurycleia, and Eumaeus been given in several books we could believe that these various introductions belonged to independent songs; but it is hard to believe that there was a group of such independent songs, that the same actor should appear in several songs, but by accident no two songs give a detailed introduction of the same person. Such heroes as Achilles, Ajax, and others of the first rank were known to the poet's audience from tradition and therefore needed no formal introduction. The description Helen gave to Priam of the different leaders as viewed from the walls of Troy was not an introduction but an effort on the part of the poet to picture the regal bearing of Agamemnon or the characteristic traits of the others there described.

Even more convincing is the fact that whenever a god appears in the form of a definite and named person, a detailed description is always added unless the god appears in the form of a person who has already been described or who has previously appeared in the action of the poem. When the god does appear in the form of a person who has already been introduced, then there is no description of that person.[21] The two following examples will illustrate the principle: Poseidon in N 45 appeared to the Greeks in the form of Calchas, with no explanation of who Calchas was; but as Calchas had already

21 "Phoenix in the Iliad," *American Journal of Philology*, XXXIII, 68.

been introduced and had taken part in the action of the poem, no introduction was necessary. Iris, in the second book, came to the Trojans to warn them of the advance of the Greeks, assuming the form of Polites, the son of Priam, who sat as a picket for the Trojans, trusting in the fleetness of his feet. Polites, whose form the divinity assumed, had not been previously named, hence the detailed introduction. The fact that in all the numerous appearances of some god under human form the person whose likeness the god assumes is invariably described, unless that person has already been introduced, but, if that person has been thus introduced, no description is ever added, can not be explained on any theory of editing independent songs, but must be due to a single plan and a single author.[22]

This principle cannot be the result of mere chance or accident, for there are sixteen different persons whose form the gods assume in the Iliad alone. This law shows also that the parts or books of the poems must have been composed in much the same order as we now have them. So far as I know this principle escaped the notice of all the earlier scholars or editors, hence it is impossible to assume that Homer was rewritten by later bards or compilers to bring the songs in harmony therewith. These two facts, that people are not introduced twice and that when gods assume the forms of men, the men are always

[22] All the examples are printed in full in the *Am. Jour. of Phil.*, XXXIII, 69 ff.

described unless they have acted previously, and if they have acted previously are never described, show convincingly that the poems of Homer were conceived as wholes, and are not due to the gradual composition of independent songs, whether these songs were composed by various bards or by Homer himself.

CHAPTER VI

THE INDIVIDUALIZATION OF GODS AND HEROES

Pope begins the Preface to his translation of the Iliad with these words: "Homer is universally allowed to have had the greatest invention of any writer whatever." A part of that invention is the ability to create characters independent of their author, who speak and act as if from their own volition with no regard for the opinions or prejudices of the one who created them.

Homer and Shakespeare, beyond all others, called into being actors who speak and live in such a detached manner that we can form no justified conclusions from them in regard to the sentiments of the poets themselves. Even in Shakespeare there does not seem to be absolute detachment, for the ruin which ultimately comes to the villains in his dramas seems intended to illustrate a moral tale. In the great work of Cervantes we can trace his religious beliefs; and the story he tells of the young Moslem maiden who deserted her kind and thoughtful father because of her change of faith, shows an almost limitless intolerance in those beliefs. Most editors of Cervantes reconstruct his biography from indications found in his own writings. This is true, also, of Dante, whose works reveal his hates, his loves, and his hope,[1] so that his writings also furnish the best sources for his biography. Bunyan had the power to individualize characters, but all of them reveal the convictions of Bunyan; while in Byron the speaker is always voicing the ideas of Byron and never becomes detached. Homer, however, has so individualized his characters that they move in his poetry and live in history as independent beings, who speak their own thoughts, not Homer's, and perform their own acts. He does not attempt to justify the ways of God to man, nor to show that righteousness leads to happiness, and sin to misery and shame.

The two noblest characters of the Iliad meet their death directly or indirectly by the treachery or cruelty of the gods. Phoebus Apollo, concealed in a cloud, stole behind Patroclus and, smiting him, left him helpless in the presence of his foe. Pallas Athena came to Hector in the guise of his brother, induced him to face the antagonist by assuring him of her help, then revealed herself as a cruel impostor by treacherously helping Achilles; and she showed no mercy to the gallant warrior whom she thus lured to destruction. Though Patroclus and Hector die, Paris survives. When the story of the Iliad ends he is still in possession of Helen, free from remorse, and rather glad to be rid of his virtuous brother,

[1] Professor deSalvio, ''Dante and Medieval Heresy,'' *Romanic Review*, 1920, 239 ff.

whose nobility and speech alike reproached him.
Achilles received misery and not blessedness for
his bravery, lamenting in Hades the rash choice
he had made when he chose a short life with glory
in preference to a long and ignoble career. For
these reasons I am unable to accept the thesis of
J. Denton Snider in his really able book (*Homer's
Iliad*, p. 497) : "We have an attempt on the poet's
part to set forth the idea and the workings of a
Providential Order in the affairs of men" or in
the statement of Wood (p. 235) : "Homer's great
object was to make mankind, and especially his
countrymen, wiser and better." Similar ideas
permeate and vitiate the Homeric writings of
Gladstone. The gods whom Homer pictures are
not the gods he worshipped; they are poetic creations whom Homer adapted to his own needs
without fear and evidently without reverence.

The following illustrations will suffice to show
that the poet of the Iliad was not trying to arouse
a feeling of affection or reverence for the divine
beings. Whenever a Greek or a Trojan was
wounded or slain in battle he never uttered a word
of complaint. Patroclus died with a taunt to
Hector that he need not boast, for his days are
numbered and he will soon die at the hands of
Achilles. When Hector meets his fate he, too,
taunts Achilles with that death which is awaiting
him. Two gods were wounded in the narrative
of the Iliad, Aphrodite and Ares. When Aphrodite received a slight wound on the wrist, she

rushed from the battle, "wailing loudly," μέγα ἰάχουσα, came to Ares, told him of her terrible sufferings, λίην ἄχθομαι ἕλκος, got into his chariot in awful anguish, ἀκηχεμένη, hurried to Olympus, threw herself into her mother's arms, and told her pitiful story. Her mother tried to console her by telling a tale of the woes the gods had undergone at the hands of mortal men—that even Ares had been put in a brazen jug and been kept there for full thirteen months. This same Ares, the god of battles, appeared on the battlefield and was wounded by the human warrior, Diomede. He bellowed, ἔβραχε, as loudly as nine or ten thousand men shout in battle, then rushed to Olympus where he told his woes to father Zeus, who showed him no pity, but roundly berated him, instead. Early in the fourth book of the Iliad Zeus seemed eager to bring the war to an immediate conclusion, so that Troy might remain standing and Helen return to her home, and a general reconciliation follow. To this fair proposal Hera replied in the most bitter anger that Troy must perish and Zeus must not permit the piety of Priam and Priam's people to thwart her purposes; that, if Zeus will surrender to her vengeance a righteous people whom he loves, she, in turn, will hand over to his will the cities she loves most of all, Argos, Sparta, and Mycenae—a brutality never surpassed on earth, yet rivaled when Antony, Augustus, and Lepidus turned over their friends to be murdered in return for the privilege of slaying their foes.

This ignoble conception of the gods is uniform throughout all parts of Homeric poetry. In the first book of the Iliad Zeus is pictured as a bully in his own home, who hurled his son from the threshold of Olympus, because that son had tried to shield his mother from one of the father's savage attacks; in B Zeus beguiled Agamemnon by means of a lying dream; in Γ Aphrodite showed herself to Helen as a most base and cruel goddess; in Δ Athena induced Pandarus to violate the oaths, then assisted in bringing about his death for the very baseness of which she was the cause; in E Aphrodite and Ares played most ignoble rôles; in Ξ Zeus allowed himself to be turned from his purposes by his carnal desires and when in Υ the gods met to fight, it was a farce beneath the dignity of the most ignoble warriors of the poem. In the Odyssey again the wanderings of the hero largely depended on the anger of Poseidon, which had been aroused because Odysseus had dared to defend himself against that god's cannibal son; Athena was ever ready to lie or to deceive; and Ares and Aphrodite were as adulterous in this poem as they had been inglorious in the Iliad.

In either poem the gods could take on any form they chose; they could assume not only the character of men but the shapes of animals as well. This identity of conception is well illustrated by Athena. Twice she assumed the character of a herald, in B 280, when she assisted in bringing the Greeks to silence, and in θ 8, when she helped

Alcinous gather the people together to welcome
the stranger. Similarly, in η 20, in the guise of
a maiden carrying a pitcher, she met Odysseus
and directed him to the palace of Alcinous. In
H 59, taking the form of an osprey, she sat on a
tree and watched the combat between Hector
and Ajax. In χ 240 she looked down upon the
slaughter of the suitors as she sat, in the form of
a swallow, on a beam in the hall. The conception
of the gods is the same in all parts of both poems,
except that in a time of war the gods always seem
more in evidence and more cruel. The Homeric
gods are not superior beings who reward virtue
in others or practice it themselves. They are only
occasionally sublime and rarely deserve reverence
or affection.

We can in a rough way construct a Homeric
mythology, but we do not have the materials for
appraising the religious element in Homer. It
is fortunate for our civilization that the early
teachers and theologians of the Hebrews were
prophets and not poets. The halls of Olympus
would have resounded with peals of "Homeric
laughter" had Zeus laid down a code of laws
which contained such a sentence as: "Honor thy
father and thy mother," for all knew too well
what he had done to his own father Cronos;
or such a sentence as "Thou shalt not commit
adultery," when they all knew the scandals of
his many amours. Most of the divinities would
have been conscientious nullificationists if there

had been any interdict on lying, covetousness, and stealing. Yet in the face of these gods the Homeric Greeks honored their parents, and lived decent as well as honest lives.

No one has ever more thoroughly grasped the meaning of the Homeric gods than Pope, who gives this sensible opinion in his Preface:

If Homer was not the first who introduced the deities, as Herodotus imagines, into the religion of Greece, he seems to be the first who brought them into a machinery for poetry, and such a one as makes its greatest dignity and importance: for we find those authors who have been offended at the literal notion of the gods, constantly laying their accusation against Homer as the chief support of it. But whatever cause there might be to blame his machinery in a philosophical or religious view, they are so perfect in the poetic that mankind has been ever since contented to follow them; none have been able to enlarge the sphere of poetry beyond the limits he has set: every attempt of this nature has proved unsuccessful: and after all the various changes of time and religions, his gods continue to this day the gods of poetry.

In these few words Pope has given all that need be said about Homeric religious beliefs. Homer drew the portraits of his gods with the hand of a poet, and as poetic portraits they are still the delight and envy of poets. It is to misunderstand and to degrade the genius of the poet to appraise him as a teacher of ethics or of religion. Homer, in spite of his picture of the gods, may have been a man of simple faith, for it must be remembered that the ages in which faith seems unquestioned

are generally those in which religious beliefs are
most broadly caricatured; hence travelers to
churches erected in the early Middle Ages are
often shocked by the farcical illustrations of
Bible stories.

After having glanced at Homer's gods we shall
turn to his men. Here again Pope furnishes just
the necessary words:

> We come now to the characters of his persons: and
> here we shall find no author has ever drawn so many,
> with so visible and so surprising a variety, or given
> us such lively and affecting impressions of them. Every
> one has something so singularly his own that no painter
> could have distinguished them more by their features,
> than the poet has by their manners.

Perhaps no poet has ever created so many outstanding men and women who have passed into
the common language of the world. Helen,
Hecuba, Andromache, Penelope, each represents a different aspect of domestic life; Ajax,
Nestor, Achilles, Patroclus, Odysseus, Diomede,
Antilochus, Hector, were all warriors, yet each
stands for something distinct and individual,
something not represented by the others. These
characters do not represent types, abstract ideas,
but human beings, each with his own life and his
own problems. Nestor is not the personification
of the wisdom coming from long experience, nor
is Ajax the embodiment of brute force. They are
all men showing the weakness as well as the
strength of men.

The writers of other Greek epics whose work has survived, such as Quintus and Apollonius, seemed unable to make their characters real and individual, and Vergil notably failed in creating characters which live. "Pious" Aeneas is not regarded as a type of the virtue which the poet desired to represent, and most people feel a sort of contempt for the hero of the *Aeneid*.[2] All of Milton's characters fail to impress us, except perhaps Satan himself. Certainly Milton would not feel complimented if he knew that in his great poem, written to "justify the ways of God to man," the character of Satan should be regarded as his greatest success. This ability to individualize character is in all parts of Homer and shows itself in all his actors. He has succeeded not a whit better with Achilles and Hector than with Eumaeus, the swineherd, Nausicaa, and the Cyclops, or even with the dog, Argus. Each is a distinct creation and as worthy his creator as any of the rest.

If I were asked to pick out a single little scene which shows, as fully as a single scene can show, the measure of the poet's greatness in the sympathetic delineation of character, that scene would be the few verses in which the blinded and baffled Cyclops takes hold of the ram which is bearing to a place of safety the very man who has blinded him, and says:

[2] Macaulay on re-reading Vergil expressed himself as greatly disappointed by the inability of the poet to give human character to his actors. Trevelyan, *Life and Letters of Macaulay*, I, 329.

Dear ram, why is it that for my sake you are thus coming out of the cave the last of the flock? Never before have you been left behind by the others, but you were always the first to graze upon the tender blades of grass, you were the first to come to the streams of water, and at evening, you were ever the first to return to the fold. But now you are the very last. Can it be that you long for the eye of your master?

Homer could not create or represent this monster without creating in him that sentiment which made him yearn for companionship and made him feel that he had found sympathy in the breast of this ram. How gentle the heart of the poet who could create a feeling of pity for this cannibal Cyclops! How compassionate the poet who could also feel for a poor old neglected dog, that had yearned for his master for twenty years, then at last sees him coming home, only to die of a broken heart—broken with joy!

Others might think the choicest cameo-like description in Homer is found in the words of lamentation spoken by Briseis over the dead body of Patroclus, and in the wise comment of the poet: "Thus she spake weeping, and all the other women joined therein, apparently weeping for Patroclus, but each was really thinking of her own sorrows." No one could have failed to observe at funerals that they weep most bitterly for the dead who have in their own lives suffered the keenest bereavement. An outstanding proof of the genius of Homer is in this, that he makes no effort to withhold his great ideas for his great characters and his great occasions, and, like a man drawing water from the ocean, he has no fear of exhaustion, no need to practice thrift.

Homer's power to create and individualize character will be illustrated in detail by two persons, selected because they appear in both poems, Helen and Odysseus.

When Homer introduces Helen in the Iliad she must appear so lovely and so beautiful that it will seem worth the effort of a nation to carry on a long war for her sake, and this must be the judgment of all. But this is difficult, for there is a great diversity in what is esteemed beautiful. One admires the blonde, another the brunette, one a plump figure, another a willowy figure, so that in praising any style of beauty one must expect to meet with adverse opinion. A second difficulty which confronts the poet lies in the fact that Helen has deserted a fine husband and has long been living in adultery. Homer masters all these difficulties by making no attempt to describe her and by allowing the hearer to estimate her beauty by the effect she produces on others. Helen is hard at work with her needle when she is told that Paris and Menelaus are on the point of fighting a duel for her sake. She goes at once modestly toward the walls of the city, from which there is a view of the field and the army, and finds there the old men of Troy—men who had suffered much, men who had lost their possessions and their kindred for her sake, men too old to be moved by the sight of ordinary beauty. When these afflicted men see Helen coming toward them they have not a word of reproach, as they say to one another, "It is no wonder that the Trojans and the Greeks have long endured miseries for the sake of such a woman, since she is as fair as the immortal gods." Priam calls to her, "Dear child, come and sit near me so that you may see your former husband, your kinsmen, and your friends. For I hold you in no way to blame. It is the gods who are responsible." On hearing these reassuring words, Helen replies with humility:

Respected art thou in my sight, and greatly revered. Oh that I had chosen death before I followed thy son hither, leaving my home, my friends, my darling child, and the lovely companionship of equals! But these things were not to be, and therefore I waste away in tears. The man of whom you ask is the son of Atreus, the wide-ruling Agamemnon, both a good king and a mighty warrior, the brother-in-law of poor shameless me, if it is not all a dream.

After pointing out and naming various leaders among the Greeks, she looks throughout the army in vain for two and says:

But two chieftains of the people, Castor and Pollux, my own brothers, I cannot see. Either they did not come from divine Lacedaemon, or else they have indeed followed the army, but are unwilling to enter the ranks of the warriors, fearing the many disgraces and reproaches which are mine.

Then the poet adds: "Thus she spake, but already the life-giving earth had covered them there in Lacedaemon, in their own native land." The

pathos of the thought that her poor brothers did
not dare to join their fellows, because they could
not endure the stories of her shame, makes it hard
for anyone to censure her. In this brief introduction of Helen we see that she was not idling
her time away, but was hard at work; that she
was beautiful, so beautiful that even the men who
were sorely afflicted could not blame others for
waging a war in her behalf; that she herself was
deeply conscious of her guilt, did not put the
fault on others, and said of the brother of her
husband, the leader of the forces which were
warring to punish her own and Paris' crime, "He
is both a good king and a mighty warrior." After
such gracious words as these we, like the old men
on the walls of Troy, cannot find it in our hearts
to chide her.

This scene shows also, by the definite information which Helen has retained of the various
Greek generals, that she is a woman of intellectual
power. Helen is no silly beauty, but she is as
clever as she is fair. After Paris' fiasco in the
duel with Menelaus, she was so disgusted with him
that she would have spurned him except for the
brutal intervention and the threats of Aphrodite.
Poor Helen said to the goddess: "I cannot go to
him, it would be a shame, and all the women of
Troy would despise me forever. I am sad enough
as it is." The goddess answered: "Woman, anger
me not, lest in my rage I abandon thee, and my
wrath shall be as ruthless as my love has been

strong. I will put cruel strife between the Greeks and the Trojans, and thou thyself shalt perish by an evil fate.'' Under such great pressure, Helen can hardly be blamed for yielding. Later during that same day Hector came to the home of Paris in order that he might shame him into bravery. Helen took the blame upon herself, and came to the conclusion that perhaps, after all, she and Paris have been involved in this evil fate that she and he may in coming ages furnish a song for generations yet unborn.

After the death of Hector, when the corpse is brought home, she takes her stand beside the bier and laments him thus:

Hector, thou art the dearest to me of all the kinsmen of my husband, and Paris is my husband. He it was who brought me here to Troy. O that I had died before that day. Now twenty years have gone since I left my native land. In all these years I have heard not one harsh or cruel word from thee, and even when others of this household chided me, thou wouldst check them with thy loving kindness and thy gentle words. I in my anguish weep for thee and my ill-fated self, for no one now in Troy is kind to me and they gaze at me with angry looks.

Helen appears in but three books of the Iliad, and each time her stay is very brief. She is beautiful, full of remorse, but she thinks only of herself. When she is at work with her needle it is to embroider or weave scenes of those battles which had been fought for her sake. Even the purpose of the war was to glorify her in song, and when she weeps for Hector, she is thinking only of Helen.

Ten years elapse before we see her again. Hard as it was for the poet to create a proper atmosphere for the introduction of Helen in the Iliad, the difficulties are much increased in the Odyssey. In these ten years she has had something of a career. Paris was slain, she was taken over by Deïphobus, and then, at length, fell into the arms or the hands of her outraged husband, who after many years and much wandering brought her back to Sparta. A woman of such a past must be hard to restore to favor, but—and this is quite as serious in the sphere of beauty— she is also ten years older; thirty years have elapsed since she eloped with Paris. Homer must recreate the spell of loveliness despite her career and despite her age.

The Odyssey has the following setting for her introduction. Telemachus and a friend have come to Sparta in search of tidings of Odysseus, and Menelaus entertains them not knowing who they are. They look with wonder upon the grandeur of his palace, whereupon he tells them that all this magnificence is naught, for he has lost many friends, whose loss is indeed bitter, but there is one who, more than all beside, makes him loathe his food and sleep. That one is Odysseus, the remembrance of whose loss fills his days with sorrow. Just at this moment Helen, as beautiful as Artemis, comes into the room, attended by maidens who carry her wool and her spinning— for Helen is still the same active house-wife she was at her first appearance in the Iliad. She modestly turns toward Menelaus, asking him the names of his guests and saying that she is startled by the resemblance she observes between one of the young men and Odysseus. "This must be the boy Telemachus, whom Odysseus left a mere babe in his home, when you Achaeans went under the walls of Troy for the sake of me, poor shameless one." Helen had seen little of Odysseus, and then under difficulties, yet she marks at a glance the features of the father in the face of the son; whereas Menelaus, who had lived with Odysseus for many years and had dined and conversed with Telemachus, has failed to see the resemblance. It is then learned that one of the young men is indeed Telemachus, whereupon they all burst into tears, sad for the absence of Odysseus. Helen then throws into the bowl from which they are drinking an Egyptian drug capable of causing forgetfulness of sorrow. This drug may well have been a poetic description of the charm of her presence. Afterwards she relates an exploit of Odysseus in which she had helped him to slay many in the streets of Troy. She begins by saying: "Zeus gives good to one and evil to another, for he is all powerful," and ends with the words: "My heart was set to return home, and I bewailed that infatuation which Aphrodite had brought upon me, when she took me away from my own country, away from my child, my home, and my husband, a husband lacking in nothing, deficient neither in

wisdom nor in beauty.'' Menelaus, blissfully
nodding, exclaims, ''That is exactly right, dear
wife, you have told the truth.'' We see by this
that she is fully restored to her home and to the
affections of her husband. Menelaus then tells a
story of her cleverness, when she came up to the
wooden horse and imitated the voices of the wives
of various Achaeans, while the men inside almost
ruined the plot in their eagerness to answer her.

At her last appearance she presents a robe
to Telemachus as he is leaving Sparta for Ithaca,
''A robe for his future wife to wear, a memento
of the hands of Helen''—evidently a robe she had
made herself. Just as Telemachus is driving
away an eagle swoops down and seizes a tame
goose from the yard, while men and women run
shouting to the rescue. The eagle flies with its
prey far away to the right. Menelaus, asked
what this omen may foretell, is mute and helpless,
but Helen interprets it thus:

Listen to me and I will prophesy as the gods put it
into my mind, and as I think it will be fulfilled. Just
as this bird sweeping down from its aerie in the mountains has seized this fowl as it fed in the yard, so
Odysseus, after much wandering and many sorrows, will
return home and be avenged, or even now he may be
at home and be in the very act of bringing ruin to all
the suitors.

With these words Helen disappears never to
reappear or to speak again. She is still the same
as when, a generation earlier, a goddess had pictured her to a Trojan shepherd as ''the fairest

woman in the world.'' On each appearance Helen is industrious, self-centered, beautiful, and extremely brilliant. She sees in an instant things which Menelaus could hardly see in an hour, or could not see at all. Menelaus in the Iliad constantly needed the protection and guidance of his stronger brother, Agamemnon, and in the Odyssey he plainly echoes the sentiments of his wife. He is a kindly, generous gentleman, but he is not shrewd and he is not interesting. He must have been poor company for so clever a woman as Helen. Poor Helen, limited to his society, with no magazines and no fashion-plates, must have craved something different, and so, from pure love for excitement, she followed Paris. Homer's portrait of Helen is a perfect picture. In spite of her few and brief appearances there is hardly a more vivid and well-defined portrait in the world's literature. All the poets who have written since Homer have been unable to add permanently a single feature, or to change a single line. The Helen of the world's imagination is the Helen of Homer, and every verse which tells of her blends in making that perfect picture.

Though all we know of Helen is given in a few verses, the hero of the Odyssey is the most often seen and the most fully described of all the characters adopted or created by Homer. In the Iliad the poet makes his theme the wrath of Achilles, but Achilles is only one, although the greatest, of a large group of mighty warriors.

Diomede, Ajax, Odysseus, Patroclus, as well as
Teucer, Idomeneus, and Nestor gain immortality,
not by association with the hero, but in their own
right in that poem. Odysseus was one of the
prominent actors in that earlier poem, was called
by his own name or that of his father not less
than one hundred and thirty times, was honored
in the councils, the battles, and the games, so that
the poet of the Odyssey took a hero with whom
the audience of the Iliad was already familiar.
In the Odyssey he dominates all scenes, those
where he is present and those from which he is
absent, and the gatherings in Olympus or in
Ithaca have meaning only as they refer to him.

The first task set for Odysseus in the Iliad was
the return of the young woman Chryseis to her
father. In its execution he showed his diplomatic
skill and quickly brought back the good-will of
the priest without compromising the honor or the
dignity of his king. His adroitness in such matters made him the natural choice of the Greeks,
when, later, they sent an embassy to appease the
angry Achilles. The absolute control of himself
and his language is repeatedly shown in the
Odyssey, but especially in his speech to Nausicaa,
when he had been cast ashore, naked, on the land
of the Phaeacians. No one could have been less
presentable than was Odysseus when he first met
the eyes of the maiden, yet he spoke in such winning and dignified language as to convince her
that he was a gentleman whom she might feed,

clothe, and admit to her own city. When later he came into the presence of Alcinous and Arete, clad in the clothing Arete herself had made and which she recognized, even in this rather unheroic situation, he talked to them in such a manner that they too were convinced of his merits, and promised to send him safely home.

Odysseus had perfect control of himself and could think calmly in a crisis and on the instant. After Agamemnon had made his foolish speech in which he urged the Greeks to abandon the struggle, thinking thereby to shame them into bravery, they took him at his word and started pell-mell on a rush to the ships, eager to hasten home. All seemed lost, and the leaders were panic-stricken. But Odysseus at once saw the danger and knew how to meet it. With energetic measures, instantly applied, he changed their spirit so completely that those who a few moments before thought only of flight were now eager for the fray. Later, when he and Ajax were wrestling for a prize, he whispered to his burly opponent to make it a sham contest and to let him throw him, advice which Ajax stupidly followed. But when it came the turn of Odysseus to fall he did not reciprocate. This same cunning and self-control saved him from the cave of the Cyclops, kept his ship from the Laestrygonian harbor where all the other ships were lost, and kept him from being too early discovered when he returned, in beggar's disguise, to Ithaca. It was this same native shrewdness which made him remove the bodies of the slain Thracians from before the horses of Rhesus, lest the horses, unused to the presence of corpses, should be terrified at the strange sight and ruin his own and Diomede's adventure.

Odysseus was not, like Achilles, a rash warrior who took risks for their own sake. His bravery was tempered with caution. Hence he did not seek a battle with Hector, Aeneas, Glaucus, or Sarpedon; but in time of real need nothing could daunt him or restrain him. When Agamemnon and Diomede had been wounded and forced to retire, Odysseus did not shrink from facing the Trojans, many of whom he slew. In the Odyssey, too, he preferred to meet danger vicariously. He sent companions to find out who the Lotus-eaters were, to investigate the nature of the Laestrygonians, and to explore the island of Circe. When, however, Eurylochus returned from the haunts of Circe and reported the loss of his companions, Odysseus did not weigh the danger nor hesitate; in spite of the pleadings of Eurylochus, he set out at once and alone to rescue them.

Odysseus had an enormous appetite and seemed always ready to eat. The fact that he ate three times in one night, that night when he and Diomede made the foray on the Thracians, has caused anguish of soul to the critics. When Achilles threw off his anger after the death of Patroclus, and after his mother had brought him his new and divine armor, he was eager to begin the battle at once, but Odysseus said: "Feed the men, for food is both strength and bravery. Hungry men cannot fight." This seemed too prosaic for the high-spirited son of Thetis, who replied: "Hungry or not, let them fight! It is no time to think of food in such an hour as this." Odysseus insisted, however, that hungry troops cared little for glory. The men were fed and glory was permitted to wait. In the Odyssey he was always ready for food. Once he told Alcinous that he must excuse him from other things and let him eat, "for there is nothing more imperious than a hungry stomach, which always bids one remember it."

Odysseus allowed neither his enthusiasm nor his emotions to make him forget the main chance, and that main chance was the advantage of Odysseus. The Phaeacians gave him a banquet, setting before him a fine piece of pork. Odysseus, in order to show his esteem for Demodocus, cut off a portion for him, but the poet slyly adds: "He cut off a piece for the bard, but the larger piece he kept for himself." One of the Phaeacians, Euryalus, had deeply offended Odysseus by saying that he resembled a trader rather than an athlete. Then when the mistake was discovered he begged pardon of Odysseus, and in token of reconciliation offered him his beautiful sword with hilt of silver and scabbard of ivory. Odysseus did not tell him to keep his sword, but offered this prayer instead: "May the gods grant you prosperity and may you never miss this sword!" When the Phaeacians invited him to remain a little longer so that they might prepare a suitable gift, although he was most eager to return home, he replied: "I would gladly stay a year, if you should spend that time in getting ready a suitable gift." The Phaeacians set Odysseus ashore in his native land, while he was still asleep, and placed his gifts by his side. And the first thing he did upon awaking was to count those gifts to see if they had left him everything. When Penelope told the suitors that suitors should bring gifts and should not consume the substance of another, Odysseus sat by and grinned to think that she was trying to increase his store.

Odysseus was the favorite of Athena and her human counterpart. She aroused him to stay the flight of the Greeks in B, sent him an omen in K, helped him in the games, encouraged his son to seek tidings of him, assisted him when among the Phaeacians, was the first to meet him on his return to Ithaca, helped him slay the suitors, and brought about the final reconciliation with his people. Odysseus must have been a fine fellow, as he had the confidence and respect of his associates. He was appointed to restore the daughter to the aged priest at the beginning of the Iliad, was selected to measure the ground for the duel (Γ), and was the chosen ambassador of the Greeks to appease the anger of Achilles. Achilles referred

to him as one of those he loved the most, Diomede
selected him as his companion on the perilous
night foray, and in the foot-race his comrades
cheered him and wished him to win. This little
touch shows his popularity with the men who
knew him, and shows that he was no sneak. In
the Odyssey all the honest people loved him and
a favorite description of him was, "For he was
as kind as a father." Twenty years had not
dulled the affections of his wife nor the admiration of the elders among his people. The old
nurse, Eurycleia, the swineherd, Eumaeus, the
neatherd, Philoetius, and even the old dog, Argus,
still yearned for their kind and considerate master. Not only the members of his own household
loved him, but we learn from the lips of Nestor
and Menelaus that he was the especial object of
their deepest affections. In Homer it is the
nobility of Odysseus quite as much as his shrewdness which exalts him. The Odysseus of the
Odyssey is the Odysseus of the Iliad; in the latter
poem he is given greater prominence, but the
features are the same. In the Iliad we have him
as a part of a group, while in the Odyssey we have
a "close-up picture" of the same hero.

The Homeric unity of character shown in
Helen and Odysseus appears equally distinct in
Nestor, Penelope, Ajax, Patroclus, Menelaus, or
in any of the rest. Each actor is consistent
throughout and each shows marks and traits
found only in himself. How did this unity arise?

Those who deny unity to Homer and who assume a multitude of authors for the Homeric poems say that these characters were created by tradition and that the unity is due to various poets working under a common impulse to a common end. We have a tradition of Odysseus outside of Homer, a tradition fairly consistent and appearing not only in the epic cycle but in the drama as well. In this un-Homeric tradition Palamedes won such fame at Troy that Odysseus from jealousy resolved to destroy him. With this in mind he had a letter written to Palamedes as if from Priam, then had it concealed in the victim's tent, whereupon he accused him of treason and urged that the tent be searched. The letter was found, the treason established, and poor Palamedes was put to death. Another tradition was that Palamedes was told that there was much hidden treasure in a well, and he was induced to go down in search of it. Odysseus and Diomede then threw stones into the well and thus slew him. In the *Ajax* of Sophocles this same Odysseus is pictured as an Iago of villainy who brought about the madness and the suicide of the great Ajax, son of Telamon, and in the *Philoctetes* of Sophocles he avows his own baseness and duplicity before the helpless invalid, but becomes a coward when that invalid has control of his bow. Tradition did, in a measure, create an Odysseus, but it is not the Odysseus of Homer. The Odysseus of tradition is hardly more than the personification of cunning and cruelty. There is nothing in this Odysseus which would make his companions cheer him in the games and desire him to win. Homer's Odysseus is his own creation.

There is rarely a consistent Greek tradition. The same story may appear in as many different forms as there are men to tell it. Each of the three great writers of Attic tragedy, Aeschylus, Sophocles, and Euripides, wrote a play on the bringing of the lame Philoctetes from Lemnos to Troy. The oracle had foretold that Troy could not be taken without the help of the bow of this outraged archer, and the manner in which he was induced to forego his anger and to come to the help of those very leaders who had so brutally abandoned him in his wretchedness forms the plot of each of these dramas. Yet each account differs from the other two.

In Aeschylus' play Odysseus was commissioned to bring Philoctetes to Troy. He walked boldly into his presence, telling Philoctetes, who failed to recognize him, that Agamemnon and his chief foe, Odysseus, were both dead. Philoctetes was seized with a paroxysm and while he was in that condition Odysseus secured possession of the bow. As the play of Aeschylus is preserved only in fragments, a part of even this brief outline is conjectural. In the play of Euripides both Odysseus and Diomede were sent to bring Philoctetes. Odysseus came as if an exile driven out by the malice of Odysseus, who had caused the death of

Philoctetes' friend, Palamedes. A Trojan embassy meanwhile arrived and urged Philoctetes to join their side, since his own Greek countrymen had so basely deserted him. Thereupon Philoctetes swooned and was treated with great kindness by Odysseus, who finally persuaded him to forego his anger and join the Greeks. This play is also fragmentary and the plot can not be restored with confidence. In the play by Sophocles it was the youthful Neoptolemus and not Diomede who went with Odysseus, and the deception practiced by Odysseus in the versions of Aeschylus and Euripides was here the work of Neoptolemus, the son of Achilles, while Odysseus did not dare to face Philoctetes, the thing he was made to do by both the others.

In these three dramas we have the same general theme presented in three different ways by three different men, all for an audience in the Dionysiac theater, in the same city, and within a period of hardly more than fifty years. These same three tragedians wrote plays on the death of Agamemnon, of Clytaemnestra, and of Aegisthus, in which the details are quite as much at variance as they are in the story of Philoctetes. Their utter failure to give anything approaching unity of character to the several actors is clearly shown, likewise, in the manner in which they portray Electra. Each of their tragedies in which that young woman plays a leading part is fortunately preserved entire. In Aeschylus Electra comes upon the scene weeping for the loss of her father, the baseness of her mother, and most of all for the absence of her brother Orestes. When her brother returns she leaves the leadership in planning and in action to him, and he makes and executes his own designs. In this play Orestes slays both his own mother and her paramour, Aegisthus. The famous recognition scene is based on the hair and the footprints of the young man. In Sophocles Electra maintains the leadership throughout, even after Orestes' return. He is only secondary. It is Electra who is the dominant character and who decides her own course as well as her brother's. Again in Aeschylus, Aegisthus is the first to be slain and Clytaemnestra knows that she too is doomed when she learns of his death. In the *Electra* of Sophocles, Clytaemnestra is murdered first and Aegisthus is led to believe that her corpse is the corpse of Orestes. When he looks at the face he sees that he has been deceived and realizes that his own doom is at hand, and this doom immediately follows. In the *Electra* of Euripides, Electra is no longer an occupant of the palace, but the wife of a peasant, and she summons her mother, pretending that she is about to give birth to a child. Meanwhile Orestes in the guise of a Thessalian traveler has slain Aegisthus, and the corpse is brought to the farm to Electra. Clytaemnestra comes in answer to the summons of her daughter, and is slain by the thrust of a sword driven by both Orestes and Electra. In this play Electra recognizes her brother not by his hair or his feet, but by a scar over the eye. Electra in the play of Euripides is coarse and cruel, entirely unlike the Electra of either of the other dramatists.

These dramas show clearly that the Greeks were not offended either by diversity in treatment of the same story or of the same character, and we are justified in believing that they would never have rewritten or revised Homer in order to make Homer's actors or Homer's stories uniform throughout. This lack of uniformity in the picture of Electra as portrayed by the tragedians is exactly like the various pictures of King David in different parts of the Bible. The books of *Samuel* and the *Chronicles* are by common consent traditional books. In *Samuel* David is described as a lustful and cruel king, who took wives from their husbands and even caused the death of one of his subjects for the sake of the possession of his wife. But when *Chronicles* pictures the reign and life of David that monarch has not a single fault. He is a king ruling in purity and righteousness—a totally different picture of the same man.[3] The most superficial study of the four gospels which tell the story of the life of Jesus will show that each one of these writers saw Jesus in a different way from all the others. These accounts are not contradictory; they were written from different points of view.

[3] I owe this remark about David to Professor F. C. Eiselen.

This total inability of two writers to see the same characters in the same way is finely illustrated by the history of the story of Don Quixote. After the appearance of the First Part and its great popularity, a clever writer undertook to continue the story and published what was assumed to be the Second Part, but he failed so completely in catching the spirit of Cervantes or in making his knight like the original that the attempt was an utter failure. Schiller and Goethe also were men of genius of high order. They lived much together and knew each other's modes of thought. Schiller communicated to his friend the outlines of a play, even the details of the plot, but he did not live to finish it. Goethe undertook to carry out the idea in the spirit of Schiller, but he found that it could not arouse his genius, that he could not get into the spirit of his friend, and he felt it necessary to abandon the attempt.[4]

It is well-known that the Greek tragedians repeated the same theme continually. The identical titles of many plays reappear in the lists of the works of the different writers, yet in Homer no scene and no story is repeated. I do not refer to mere repetitions by messengers or to summaries, such as Achilles' words to his mother, or the account Telemachus gave of his journey. All the characters in Homer are uniform, they have life and individuality, but no scene from the Iliad is repeated in the Odyssey. The same

[4] Referred to by Rothe, *Odyssee als Dichtung*, 202.

audience in Athens could see the same person represented in entirely different and contradictory aspects and could hear the same story retold with different features and with different actors. Who gave this unity to Homeric characters and who kept the same story from being retold? Certainly not a group of men who felt no shock at hearing contradictions and at seeing repetitions. Who gave the poetry of Homer this unity of character and this unity of action? There is but one answer: The unity of character which pervades the poetry of Homer must be due to the fact that each actor sprang from a single brain, a brain which pictured each individual with such vividness and such distinctness that incongruity and contradictions were impossible. These clear and distinct outlines are the creation of a single mind; they are not a composite picture by several masters. In all composite pictures the centers are fairly distinct, the edges are blurred and confused. It is the clearness of the edges which proves the unity of Homer.

This unity of character is expressed in a style which stands entirely alone. Matthew Arnold said of this style: "Homer has not Shakespeare's variations. Homer always composes, as Shakespeare composes at his best. The compelling argument for Homeric unity is that the poem has the magic stamp of a master and that stamp is the grand style."[5] A critic so competent and a

[5] *On Translating Homer,* Lecture II.

poet so great as Shelley said: "As a poet Homer must be acknowledged to excel Shakespeare in the truth, the harmony, the sustained grandeur, the satisfying completeness of his images."[6] Greek hexameters were written for a thousand years and more after Homer, but none of these hexameters remind us of him. We never, except to glorify him, think of Homer, when we read Hesiod, Apollonius, Quintus, or Nonnus, yet all of them wrote in his meter and in his dialect. All the great mass of poetry known as the epic cycle seems to have been composed in something like the Homeric manner and on themes resembling Homer's themes. Still no one has ever quoted a single verse nor referred to a single scene from any poem of the entire cycle as illustrating either high merit or poetic excellence. It is beyond credulity to suppose that a group of poets should all have written in the same grand style, that all their work should have been collected into the Iliad and the Odyssey, and that by chance not another poet whose works accidentally fell to any other poem should have attained that style. The one poet whom we know who lived closest to the time of Homer is Hesiod, and we are positively certain that the author of the *Works and Days* could have written no one of the great scenes of either the Iliad or the Odyssey.

It is easier to believe that Shakespeare wrote *King Lear, Macbeth, Hamlet, Othello,* and *The Merchant of Venice* than that five men lived at that

[6] Quoted by Professor Smyth, *Columbia Lectures on Greek Literature,* 46.

time, each capable of writing one of these plays. *Hamlet* is the best possible evidence of Shakespeare's ability to write *Othello*. No other poet known to us was capable of writing the story of the ransom of the body of Hector except that poet who wrote also the parting of Hector and Andromache, the speeches of the embassy, the death of Hector, and the story of the Phaeacians. Other writers might suggest Homer but no one of them could be mistaken for him. They could paraphrase him, parallel him, imitate him, but they have produced nothing which posterity has cared to place by the side of any of his great scenes. They might at times seem to catch the spirit of Homer, but they did not. They have enriched the world with no Nausicaa, no Eumaeus, and no Andromache.

[Dr. Heinrich Spiess in his *Menschenart und Heldentum in der Ilias* suggested to me the idea of writing this chapter. I owe much to him for many suggestions.]

CHAPTER VII

HECTOR

When Herodotus gave an account of the great series of struggles by which the Greeks drove out of Europe the forces of Asiatic despotism, he said that the purpose of his narrative was to preserve to the glorious actions of the Greeks and of the barbarians their due meed of praise. This eagerness to preserve the glory of his enemies as well as that of his own countrymen was peculiarly Greek. Thucydides was the historian of that terrible war in which Athens lost her empire to the forces of Sparta, yet so impartially is the story told that except for one or two chance references it might be argued that the author was not an Athenian, for a Spartan general, Brasidas, seems to have been his favorite. This ability to humanize the foe was entirely unknown to the Hebrew writers. Their enemies never appealed to their sympathies, and the various inhabitants whom they dispossessed of their homes seem never to have touched the pity nor to have aroused the better emotions of any of the sacred writers.

Herodotus and Thucydides, in this impartiality and in their appreciation of the virtues of their foes, were followers of Homer, who so graciously entered into the heart and the nobler sentiments of the enemy that it was a Trojan, not a Greek, who became the moral hero of the poem. Yet Homer was a Greek with all the sympathies and prejudices of a patriotic Greek. He never pictures any of his countrymen as begging for life or as taken prisoner; the death of a Greek is always avenged, the death of a Trojan but rarely; and generally, when a Trojan falls, his name is given, but the slain Greeks are for the most part nameless.[1] The Greeks advance to battle with perfect discipline and in quiet, while the Trojans move with confusion and tumult. The short victory which came to the Trojans was made necessary because of the determination of Zeus to honor Achilles. Even the Trojan success, therefore, was for the purpose of giving greater glory to a Greek. The Trojans were at war because of the violation of the sacred obligations of guest-friendship, and hostilities were renewed by the treacherous wounding of Menelaus by Pandarus in defiance of most solemn oaths. Against this background of violated hospitality and perjured oaths Homer drew the character of Hector.

In the early part of the poem this hero of the Trojan forces is not brought upon the stage nor given prominence. Long before we see him, however, we know that he is to be the chief antagonist, the one whom the Greeks are most to fear.

[1] Frey, ''Hektor,'' Bern *Program* 1895. There were slain 189 named Trojans and 53 named Greeks. Hector slew 28 of these Greeks.

Achilles in his anger swore that the Greeks would rue his absence on that day when many should fall at the hands of man-slaying Hector. Also, Agamemnon called the leaders of the Greeks together for sacrifice and prayed that Zeus grant him the power of burning that very day the halls of Priam and of bringing vanquished Hector to the dust. By the words of Achilles and the prayer of Agamemnon the poet was able to create the impression that Hector was a known and illustrious warrior. We are not surprised therefore to find that, when the Trojans are first introduced, it is Hector on whom chiefly rests the protection of the city, nor to read in the Trojan Catalogue that "Great Hector of waving plume, the son of Priam, led the Trojans, and with him the best warriors eagerly armed themselves."

When the opposing forces at last moved forward, as if to begin the struggle, Paris advanced in front of his own army challenging the best of the foe to meet him in single combat. At once Menelaus sprang forward, eager to avenge himself on the defiler of his home, whereupon Paris drew back, terrified, into the ranks of the Trojans. Then Hector upbraided him with the words: "Wretched Paris, fairest of form, woman-mad, deceiver, would thou hadst never been born and hadst died unwed." He bitterly reproached him for his folly and his cowardice, and ended with the biting taunt: "But the Trojans are timidly lenient, or else ere this hadst thou put on a tunic of stone, for the ills thou hast wrought." These were the first words spoken by Hector. They show in advance that he had no sympathy for the course pursued by Paris and no heart in the war. Paris was driven to renew the challenge, and the duel was prepared on the condition that the winner should take Helen and all her possessions, the Trojans continue to live in Troy, and the Greeks return to their own country. Hector was determined to bring peace at any price. He felt that the war was founded on dishonor.

Paris proved a poor champion. He was rescued from the fight by Aphrodite, and Menelaus was left alone, a victor, on the field of honor. Then Pandarus, a Trojan ally, treacherously wounded Menelaus, the solemn oaths were violated, and the Trojans added to their infamy by rushing to battle and making the treachery of Pandarus their own. The Trojan cause was thus loaded with a double guilt: the rape of Helen and the baseness of Pandarus.

The first mention we have of Hector in the battle that ensued is in the verse, "The Trojan leaders drew back, even the mighty Hector fled." It is highly suggestive that at the first appearance of this champion on the field, he should be in retreat. It was he who had shamed Paris into playing the man; it was he who had conducted the negotiations which led to the truce and the oaths. But, outraged by the conduct of Paris and the treachery of his own people, his spirit was

gone and he had not the heart to fight. The
Greeks seemed on the point of winning, even
without the help of Achilles, when Sarpedon
shamed Hector into action. He accused him of
enticing the allies to undertake the struggle for
Troy and the Trojans while he himself stood
basely aside, neither fighting nor inspiring others
with valor. Hector made a feeble effort to play
the man, but he did not enter the fighting again
until Ares joined him and forced him into the
struggle. The little glory he then won was not
his own; it was shared with the god of war.

Soon he dropped out of sight, and the Trojans
were on the point of retreating, when Helenus, the
seer, suddenly advised Hector to leave the battle,
go to the city, and tell his mother and the women
of Troy to appease Athena by offering gifts to
that angry goddess. Immediately he ceased fighting and made this address to his troops: "Ye
proud-spirited Trojans and ye illustrious allies,
be men and think of your impetuous courage while
I depart to Ilium that I may bid the elders and
the women to offer sacrifices to the immortal
gods." Thereupon he left his hard-pressed men.
Surely it was an astounding thing for a champion
to leave his men in the moment of greatest danger,
that he might himself carry a simple message.
He might have sent Helenus with orders to repeat
in the city the advice Helenus had just given to
him, or he might have sent the least important
person in the army. It was a poetic, not a mili-

tary, consideration, which induced Homer to use Hector as a messenger. He wished to present a scene from domestic life; Hector was needed for that scene and therefore was spared from the battle.

The account of his mission to the city, his meeting with his mother, the contrast between him and Paris, the words with Helen, and, above all, the scene between the wife, the husband, and the little son, is generally regarded as the very greatest triumph of literary genius. The words with which Hector addressed his wife are very significant: "This I know in heart and soul that a day will come when sacred Troy shall fall and Priam and the people of Priam with good ashen spear." The sadness of these words is deepened from the fact that they are the very words spoken by Agamemnon when he perceived that Menelaus had been shot by Pandarus in defiance of the oaths. We see that Hector has no heart and no hope in the struggle, that he feels that the gods are justly against his own people.

Although this parting scene is rated as of high merit by all lovers of poetry, it is almost universally rejected by the critics as a late intrusion which destroys the effect and the harmony of the whole. That this parting scene should not be the final parting and the last farewell seems in their eyes a supreme poetic absurdity. Hector, according to the present Iliad, returned at the end of this day's fighting to his home and wife, that is, he spent the night after the parting, the night after the first day's fighting, presumably the twenty-second in the story of the Iliad, within the city. He seems also to have been in Troy most of the two following days and nights. The success of the Trojans in the second day's fighting, the twenty-fifth day of the Iliad, induced him to encamp near the place of combat and to remain outside the walls. On the following day Patroclus was slain and Achilles was kept from fighting until his mother could bring him new armor. Hector spurned the wise advice of Polydamas to return within the walls. He remained that night on the plain, and was slain by Achilles on the following day. Thus Hector died on the twenty-seventh day of the action of the Iliad, or five days after the scene of parting. Of the five intervening nights three seem to have been spent in the city, without doubt in his own home, and two outside the walls not far from the camp of the Greeks.

No doubt every reader is somewhat surprised to find that Hector and Andromache meet again after the scene of parting. The higher critics see in this account a contamination of two or more independent traditions. They believe that, in the original version, Hector parted from Andromache to meet the foe and die, and that he never saw his wife or son again. The difficulty they find is in the fact that this solemn parting is for only a few hours, while the real and final farewell is passed over in silence. Is this true to the highest and best standards of poetry? There is no truth in poetry which is not also truth in life. Most farewells in this world have, indeed, not been last farewells, and surely no husband and father ever went to dangerous battle without some such parting as this. The pathos of the scene was not changed by the accident that he may have returned though many of his companions fell.

In the story of the Bible, the first person to prepare for death by giving his final blessing to his son and successor was Isaac. In that account (Genesis xxvii: 1 ff.) Isaac said he wished to bless his son and then to die. Clearly the thought of this patriarch was that his course had been run. But he did not die; he was still alive when Jacob returned from serving Laban. Whether the story of Isaac was an actual fact or not, it was at least so regarded by the compilers and preservers of the narrative. It was no more necessary that Hector's fears should have been immediately fulfilled than that Isaac's blessing should have been followed by his death. After Hector had left his wife and had met Paris, the natural reaction set in and he told Paris what they would do when finally they were rid of the Greeks. Here he was mistaken, for he never lived to "drink a cup of freedom in his halls."

When Socrates was condemned to death he said to those who condemned him, "I wish to prophesy to you, for I am now at that point where men especially foretell the future, when they are about to die." He then predicted that certain things would happen which never came to pass. The signal failure of this prophecy changed in no particular the impressive solemnity of the utterance. Would the grief of Penelope during those twenty years have been more bitter if at the end Odysseus had not returned? We can look at the outcome and anticipate sorrow or comfort thereby, but Penelope, Hector, and Andromache could not. The poet chose to paint their feelings rather than ours. This, it seems to me, is the essence of the whole matter: the poet preferred to picture the emotions of the actual participants in the action of the poem rather than those of the hearer or the reader.

Homer has such a perfect parallel to this parting scene and its delayed fulfillment that it is strange these disintegrators overlooked it. The parting of Calypso and Odysseus is, on her part at least, closely akin to the one in the sixth book of the Iliad. How a modern poet would view this scene and where he would put it is illustrated by Stephen Phillips' *Ulysses*. In that play the passionate farewells are spoken on the shore. During their utterance Ulysses embarks, speaking his final words from the deck of the moving ship, which slowly fades from the sight of the distracted goddess. Where does Homer place the scene of these farewells? The story is found in the fifth book of the Odyssey. When Hermes warns Calypso that Zeus has decreed that Odysseus is to leave her, the goddess reluctantly seeks him out and tries eagerly to induce him to remain with her and to become immortal; but, failing in this, she bids him farewell: σὺ δὲ χαῖρε καὶ ἔμπης— as beautiful and dignified words of parting as were ever spoken! We expect these to be her last words and that Calypso and Odysseus will part at once. But he does not leave. Instead he follows her to her home, then for four days he works at his raft under her direction, and on the fifth he sails away without either of them speaking another word of farewell. It seems too deadly a parallel even to draw it, to say that Hector and Andromache bade farewell, that he was slain on the fifth day thereafter, and that the last parting was in silence; and that Odysseus and Calypso bade farewell, that he parted on the fifth day thereafter, and that the last parting was in silence.

That one died on the fifth day, and the other parted on the fifth day after the farewells were spoken can hardly be more than an accident. The fact that neither parting scene was put at the moment of the last meeting must be no accident but poetic design. No careful student of Homer can fail to grasp the poetic purpose in this. The poet constantly avoids scenes of too much tragic pathos or too great emotional intensity. When Hector met his death at the hand of Achilles, the wife was not a witness of that scene, although it was enacted in full view of the walls. She was busy with her work in her own room, and at the

very moment he was slain she was taking pride
in a piece of artistic embroidery which she was
then finishing. What an opportunity the poet had
to place Andromache on the walls and "to tear
a passion to tatters"! The poet shows his com-
posure in the fact that we never hear the lamenta-
tions of the wounded and the dying, and no soldier
raises himself to his knees and breaks the death
sobs and groans by some tearful message to father
or to mother. If the scene of parting in either
case had been put at the moment of greatest
danger or of intensest emotion it would have violated that fine and dignified feeling which Homer
everywhere observes. The placing of the parting
words of Hector and Andromache and of Odysseus and Calypso long before the last and final
farewell is a perfect example of the Homeric and
Hellenic reserve which is best expressed by the
phrase, μηδὲν ἄγαν, ("nothing too much"), and
which induced the great Attic orators to close
their speeches with calmest utterances. The same
unerring poetic judgment shows itself in the parting of Hector and Andromache and in the parting
of Odysseus and Calypso.

Just at the moment when the Trojans seemed
on the point of victory an eagle appeared on the
left with a live snake in its talons. The snake
kept striking the neck and breast of its captor
until the eagle was forced to drop it and fly away,
while the snake fell and squirmed within the ranks
of the Trojans. The superstitious Polydamas

immediately interpreted the omen as an order from Zeus to stop the battle, even though the battle was apparently hastening to so successful an issue. This advice of Polydamas was wonderfully like that given to Nicias, with such terrible results, so many centuries later in the harbor of Syracuse. Hector could not leave the battle for the sake of a bird and a snake, and he angrily replied to the seer: "You bid me put my trust in wide-winged birds; I care not for them and I heed them not, whether they move toward the right and the rising sun or toward the left and the regions of darkness. One omen is best, to fight for native land." This utter break with the superstitions of his people must have shocked many, who were now terrified both by the omen and by Hector's evident want of faith. It is hard to grasp how modern this sentiment of Hector is and to remember that, centuries after Homer, great generals moved their armies according to the aspect of the liver of the sacrificial victims. Later Hector inspired his discouraged men with these splendid words:

Fight all of you beside the ships and if any falls pierced with a javelin or thrust with a spear, may he meet his end knowing that it is glorious to fall fighting for one's native land, for then his wife and his children shall remain in safety, when the Greeks have fled home in their ships.

When, at last, Achilles, the son of a goddess, and protected by divine armor, came on the field, Hector knew that he was no match for him; but his sense of honor and his love for his country would not permit him to seek his own safety back of the walls of the city. Achilles shouted to him: "Come nearer that you may the sooner find your death." Hector without any illusions and without fear replied: "Son of Peleus, do not hope to frighten me with hard speech as if I were a child, since I too am able to utter coarse and reviling words. I know that thou art a mightier warrior and that thou art stronger far than I." The greatness and the sadness of the course followed by Hector lay in this: that he was the champion of a cause which was distasteful to him, fighting a foe whom he regarded as his superior, and, most pathetic of all, he could not hope for the sympathy of the gods in a cause which he himself condemned. He was in the war solely as a defender of his family and his state. For these he urged others to die and for them he himself gave his life. No other character in Homer resembles Hector in the motives which led him to action or in the gentle forgetfulness of self in his anxiety for others. It is a strange touch of the poet's genius that the last words spoken in regard to Hector should be from the lips of Helen, who had deserted her own home and who thought of others only in relation to her own happiness.

The breadth of the poet's sympathies is shown in the last verse of the Iliad: "Thus then they buried Hector the knight." The first verse of the poem named Achilles the Greek; the last verse, Hector the Trojan.

Hector has the distinction of being the only person who is named in every one of the twenty-four books of the Iliad. Not even Achilles shares in this honor, since Achilles is not referred to directly or indirectly in the third book. Agamemnon, the Greek leader, is not mentioned in books twelve, twenty, and twenty-one. Though Hector is named in every book of the Iliad, he is not referred to in a single book of the Odyssey. He is solely the actor of a single poem and in that poem he is all important. Without a Hector the plot of the Iliad has no existence. There is no doubt that the character of Hector, with his seeming boldness and reputation so out of all proportion to his actual achievements, is at first sight extremely baffling. Mahaffy regards "the character and position of Hector as the strongest and clearest inconsistency in the entire Iliad."[2] He tries to bring harmony by assuming that, in the original Iliad, Hector was superior to all the Greeks excepting only Achilles, and he assumes that his various discomfitures before Ajax, Diomede, and the rest were added by bards to glorify these different Greeks at the expense of the original renown of Hector.

Wilamowitz, throughout his *Die Ilias und Homer,* assumes that Hector has been taken over from some previous epic written exclusively in his honor, and he has named this poem *Das Hektorgedicht.* His contention is that the redactor of the Iliad took fragments from this epic

[2] *History of Greek Literature,* I, 87.

and fitted them into the present poem. The
simple fact that Hector is named in every book
of the Iliad shows how essential he is to the plot
and that without him there would be little action.
If there ever was an original poem with Hector
as its protagonist, it must have been written by
a Greek bard to delight a Greek audience. Such
a thing is no more probable than that a Spanish
bard should have sung to Spanish audiences the
glories of Drake, or that French bards should
have delighted the people of France with the
glorious exploits of the Crown Prince of Germany.
I know that the Serbian bards sing of their own
defeats at Kossovo, but it is in honor of their own
leaders, and not to glorify the leaders of the
Turks. A certain amount of praise for Hector
was entirely proper from a Greek bard and before
a Greek audience when, at the end, even that hero
falls before a greater champion of their own.
But a Greek song devoted exclusively to setting
forth the glories of Hector and the discomfiture
of the Greeks would have been an impossibility.
Even when Hector is most valiant and achieves
the most, we feel that he is a tethered hero, and
that the poet resents his winning any glory at
the expense of the Greeks. Generally a god is
by his side; or the god really vanquishes the
foe and then allows the glory to Hector. For,
although Achilles puts on Hector all the blame
for the loss of Patroclus, it was really Apollo
who deserved that glory.

Bethe,[3] following Dümmler,[4] has advanced the theory that most of the heroes of the Iliad were transferred to that poem from other songs or ballads and that in those original songs they had nothing to do with Troy. He argued that Hector was at one time a Theban hero and the fact that he appeared as fighting at Troy might be explained by the assumption that the original traditions of Hector were connected with a Troy in Attica and were later transferred to the Troad. This assumption is based on the fact that there was a late tradition that Hector's grave was to be found at Thebes. Information in regard to the grave of Hector is given in a scholium to N 1:

> For the Thebans being beset by misfortunes consulted the oracle in regard to a release, and the oracle told them that their woes would cease if the bones of Hector should be brought from Ophrynium of the Troad and buried in Thebes at a place designated by the oracle. They did this and their troubles ceased.[5]

If Hector had really been a Theban hero, this must have been known from earliest times and would have been mentioned by Theban writers. We are fortunately able to test Theban traditions by the writings of two early poets, Hesiod and Pindar. Hesiod outranks in point of antiquity any other writer except Homer, and Pindar, in the matter of time, has but few rivals. When to Pindar's antiquity is added the fact of his great

---

[3] *Neue Jahrbücher,* VII, 657, XIII, 1.

[4] Studniczka, *Kyrene,* Anhang II.

[5] This oracle and scholium are discussed by Radtke, *Hermes* XXXVI, 35.

wealth of myth and of traditional allusions, he must be regarded as the very highest authority for all ancient traditions, especially those in any way connected with Thebes. These two poets, Hesiod and Pindar, are not only ancient, but, what is of far more importance in the present matter, they are strikingly independent of Homer, since they not only give vast stores of tradition not found in Homer, but even unhesitatingly contradict him.[6] We are confident therefore that in coming to these poets we come to uncontaminated sources and that respect for Homer will not have dried up the springs of Theban tradition in regard to Hector.

Hector is never mentioned in any of the poetry assigned to Hesiod. The one Trojan warrior whom he names is Aeneas. He tells how Aeneas was conceived on the slopes of Mt. Ida, that is, Aeneas did not belong to a European, but to an Asiatic Troy. Hesiod, moreover, places in the Islands of the Blest those warriors who had gone in ships over the sea to recover the fair-haired Helen. This reference is most instructive, for it shows what the tradition was in European Greece. If it be granted that the Greek colonists or exiles took their old songs with them and substituted new names for the old, putting an Asiatic Troy where once an Attic Troy had been, how are we to account for the fact that back there in the

[6] "Hector as a Theban Hero in the Light of Hesiod and Pindar," *Am. Jour. of Phil.*, XXXV, 309 ff.

I have elsewhere discussed the independence of Homer as shown in Hesiod and Pindar ("A Comparative Study of Hesiod and Pindar," Johns Hopkins University dissertation, 1897).

old home a Bœotian poet is singing of that same
Asiatic Troy? Had Hesiod lived a few centuries
later we could say that he was influenced by
Homer; but we cannot accept that answer for a
poet of marked independence of Homer, and who
was almost if not quite a contemporary. Hesiod
does not afford the slightest presumption that
Hector in his day was regarded as a Theban hero.

Pindar regarded Hector with unusual affection and admiringly called him the "invincible
and steadfast pillar of Troy." It is beyond doubt
that this Troy was not in Attica but was the Troy
of Asiatic Troad, for Pindar tells how glory
bloomed for Hector by the waters of the Scaman-
der. This poet mentions Hector by name no less
than six times, yet he never suggests that he was
in any way connected with Pindar's Thebes. He
always makes him the defender and the glory of
Asiatic Troy. Can any one in the face of this
significant fact assert that Pindar knew that at
one time this much admired Hector was the support of his own beloved but ill-starred Thebes and
that he suppressed that knowledge in silence?
The knowledge of traditions shown in the works
of Pindar proves that he would have known such
a tradition if there had been one. The silence of
Pindar in regard to a Theban Hector is therefore
absolute proof that Hector was not then regarded
as having any connection with Thebes. Not only
does Pindar sing of no Hector except the Trojan
Hector, but, what is far more important, he has

no knowledge of that Hector except as he found it in Homer. It is easy to put one's finger on some passage in the Iliad which justifies and explains every Pindaric reference to Hector. Pindar was no docile follower of Homer, as I have already shown. Besides differing from Homer, he often adds details not mentioned in the Iliad. For example (*N.* III, 52), he tells how Achilles, because of his unusual fleetness of foot, captured deer without nets or dogs. This is a touch not founded on Homer, yet in harmony with the phrase "the swift-footed Achilles." Pindar adds no lines and gives no new features to the Homeric picture of Hector. The problem of Hector lies right at the heart of the Iliad. That hero has had no part in any previous "Hektorgedicht," nor in any exploits connected with Thebes. The first and only poem to give a portrait of him was the Iliad.

In the first thousand lines of the Iliad, Achilles, Agamemnon, Telamonian Ajax, and the other Ajax, the son of Oïleus, Idomeneus, Diomede, Nestor, Menelaus, Calchas, and Patroclus are introduced. The prominent Greek actors are marched across the stage at the very start; then when, in later scenes, they have played their parts, they reappear at the games, make their farewell bows, and disappear with no trace of bitterness from the "wrath" and no scars from their wounds. They are thus restored to the condition in which they were before the "wrath" began. Evidently Homer had the conception of the

Greek heroes distinctly in mind from the start.
Tradition for the most part had furnished their
names and had already settled the fate of each.
Agamemnon could not die in battle, for his death
was reserved for his return. Odysseus, Diomede,
Nestor, and Menelaus must not fall at Troy, since
their home-coming was a settled part of the epic
saga; nor could any warrior win glory by slaying
Ajax. The Greek leaders, as well as the fate
of each, were already fixed by their own tradition,
which, passing on from one generation to the
next, would be definite and exact on the Greek
side, but most vague and deficient concerning
the Trojans. Homer had no knowledge of the
Trojans except as Greek pride or patriotism preserved it. Although the Greek leaders pass in
review at once and we know who are to be the
actors in subsequent events, there is no similar
introduction of the Trojans. Except Hector and
Priam, who are casually referred to in the first
book, the Trojans are named only when they act.
Paris does not enter and we have no inkling of
his connection with the war until he meets Menelaus in the duel. Aeneas, Glaucus, Sarpedon,
appear first in E, Helenus makes his initial bow
in Z, Dolon in K, Polydamas in Λ; Coön, who forces
Agamemnon to withdraw, and Socus, who wounds
Odysseus, both win glory and death at their first
appearance. Even Euphorbus, destined to have
the great honor of wounding Patroclus, is not
named previous to that exploit. The poem is

manifestly written from the point of view of the Greeks; the Trojans are introduced or created merely that the Greeks may have antagonists.

Homer appears at his weakest in finding names and exploits for the Trojans. Tradition, Greek tradition, had supplied him with very few foreign names, and so, accordingly, nearly all the Trojans are fitted out with good Greek names. In book four is mentioned a Greek by the name of Chromius, then in later books four Trojans appear bearing that same name. One Greek and three Trojans have the Greek name Melanippus, one Greek and two Trojans are called Antiphus, two Trojans have the name Adrastus, two Astynous, two Ennomus, two Ophelestes, two Pylartes, two Thersilochus, and more than a score of the Trojans, such as Alastor, Medon, Noëmon, Orestes, are identical in name with some Greeks of the poem. Tradition failed also to give Homer the name of Hector's wife, else she had not appeared with the Greek name Andromache. The same is true of his son Astyanax, as well as of his half-brothers and brothers, Deïphobus, Helenus, Polydorus, Polites, Antiphonus, and Agathon.

Paris is the only one of the Trojan leaders who has an undisputed foreign name. It seems unlikely that tradition could have preserved the name of the son and forgotten the name of the father; hence the tradition found in Apollodorus (II, 6, 4), that Priam was at one time known as Podarces, is probably to be accepted as showing that the Greeks regarded Priam as a foreign name, which they rendered in their own speech with Greek equivalents. If Hector ever had the Trojan name Darius, Homer gives no hint that he knew it, and Hector never appears in Homer except under this good Greek name. Even had tradition told how a foreign prince with a foreign name sailed to Greece to entice Helen, it had not given the names of his companions. Accordingly the poet had the ship built by a Greek Phereclus, the son of the Greek, Tecton, whose sire in turn also was a Greek, Harmon. Hector, in name, dress, character, and all, is a Greek loaned to the enemy; by these same tokens Paris is foreign throughout.

My explanation for all the difficulties involved in an appreciation of the parts played by Hector and Paris in the action of the Iliad is this: Paris was the traditional leader and champion of the Trojans, but for moral reasons could not be made the protagonist in the poem. The poet therefore degraded him and created a hero with sufficient nobility of character to win sympathy for his cause. Hector, as he appears in Homer, is the creation of the poet who conceived the idea of the Iliad; without Homer there would have been no traditions of Hector.

The place of Paris in tradition and in Homer will be first considered. We know little of the contents of the Cyclic poems, yet we learn that Paris was the leading actor of the *Cypria,* that he was a person of sufficient importance to be called upon

to decide the contest of the goddesses, that he took
a fleet to Greece to secure Helen, and that on his
return he was able to pillage the wealthy city of
Sidon. All of this is in harmony with the Iliad,
even if not definitely expressed. The deeds of no
other Trojan find any place in the story of the
Cypria. The phrase found in the summary of
this poem "and Protesilaus died at the hands
of Hector" is not an independent tradition, but
is founded on the Iliad and in plain violation of
Homer, as will appear later. In the *Aethiopis*
Achilles is slain by Paris with the aid of Apollo.
No other Trojan is named in the *Chrestomathia*
of Proclus as sharing in the events of this poem.
In the *Ilias Parva* Paris is slain by Philoctetes,
who has just come from Lemnos. Even here
Paris is not slain as a coward or in flight, but is
bold enough to face Philoctetes in a duel. No
other Trojan has a part in that poem, except
Helenus, who like a traitor informs the Greeks
how his own city may be taken. Thus we find
that in the first three poems of the Cycle, leaving
the Iliad out of account, Paris is the only Trojan
whose acts are of sufficient importance to receive
mention in the summary by Proclus. Paris alone
of the Trojans had the honor of causing the death
of a Greek leader, and that leader was none other
than Achilles himself.

The character of Paris in the Iliad involves
constant contradictions. The first great contradiction is that he who had proved himself to be

such a craven and a coward should be introduced as "Alexander the godlike." Why this honoring name? The scholiast to M 93 says that Paris was called Alexander since he defended his fatherland when the foe came against it. Evidently the honoring titles, "divine," "godlike," "royal Alexander," which at first glance seem so inappropriate in Homer, are in complete harmony with pre-Homeric traditions. The second contradiction is found in the fact that a Greek, with his feeling that to be beautiful is also to be brave, καλὸς καὶ ἀγαθός, should have represented a coward as handsome. Paris is the "fairest in form" and because of his beauty the Greeks at once drew the conclusion that he was the Trojan champion. It was the physical defects in Thersites on which the poet placed the greatest emphasis, and Homer had a real difficulty in representing the handsome figure of Paris in the guise of a poltroon, capable of the ignoble part he played in the third book. A third contradiction is found in the continued influence of Paris. After fleeing from Menelaus and disgracing himself and his cause, he should have had but little influence or power. Yet on the evening of that very day, when Antenor made the inevitable suggestion that the oaths be kept and Helen with her possessions be returned to the Greeks, Paris arose and insultingly refused to consider the idea of returning Helen. Hector was mute, no one answered, and the herald was sent to report to the Greeks the decision of Paris. The power of Paris was so out of keeping with his character that Herodotus (ii, 120) could only explain this contradiction by assuming a tradition according to which Helen had never been in Troy, but was detained in Egypt; otherwise Hector, in spite of Paris, would have delivered her to the Greeks. It is also to be noted that, though the other married sons of Priam lived in the same palace with their father (Z 242), Paris had a palace all his own.

Paris is no coward in Homer and no weakling. His heroic proportions show through, despite the efforts of the poet to paint him as a mean and timorous warrior. This is shown by the fact that he and not Hector determined the decision of the assembly, and by the following chance details: Paris was a leader of one of the larger divisions of the Trojans (M 93). When Aeneas was sore pressed by the Greeks he sought help, "trying to fix his eye on Paris" (N 490). In the very thick of the contest Hector was much encouraged by finding Paris "arousing his companions and urging them to fight." (N 766.) Moreover, it was the skill and bravery of Paris (Λ 504) that saved to the Trojans the fighting of the third day's struggle.

Only one Greek of any importance was slain in the action of the Iliad, and comparatively few were wounded. Paris was the only Trojan to wound a Greek of the first rank who was not himself slain. Euphorbus and Hector, who caused the death of Patroclus, Pandarus, who wounded Menelaus, Coön, who pierced Agamemnon, and Socus, who stabbed Odysseus, paid for their brief glory with their lives. But Paris, without divine aid, wounded Diomede, Machaon, and Eurypylus, slew Euchenor, Menesthius, and Deïochus; yet he himself escaped. His greatness in Homer is of a like character with that in the *Cypria, Aethiopis,* and *Ilias Parva.*

Paris was an archer, but that was no disgrace despite the anger of Diomede at being shot with an arrow. A people who regarded the ambush as the place of greatest honor (A 227) and a tradition which gave glory to such archers as Teucer and Philoctetes, or made the bow of Heracles his greatest possession, and the bow of Odysseus the arbiter of marriage—these could not have considered skill in archery a source of infamy. Paris' sole weakness was moral weakness. Great as he was in tradition and is in Homer, the false friend and adulterer could not be permitted a position of epic leadership. No people under the control of such a leader as Paris could win sympathy. Tradition furnished the Trojans with no other leader, therefore the poet must create one.

Hector has no place in the pre-Homeric tradition as given in the *Cypria.* In that poem his name is found but once, where it is said that he slew Protesilaus. Homer knew nothing of this, as his account of the death of that warrior (B 698 ff.) shows. In this passage in the Catalogue it is said that a Dardanian man slew Protesilaus. This cannot refer to Hector, since Homer never uses the word Dardanian for Trojan.[7] The author of the *Cypria*, with the plot of the Iliad before him, could not see why so important a hero as Hector had no standing in tradition outside of Homer, and so created an exploit for him by quietly removing the Homeric "Dardanian man" and substituting Hector. Here the attempt to give Hector a position in the Cycle which was not warranted by pre-Homeric tradition is evident and unmistakable.

It is a matter of common observation that many of the leaders in the events described by the Iliad have designations which have no adequate explanation in the action of the poem itself. Priam, who does not and could not wield a spear, is none the less "Priam of good ashen spear," and, though withdrawn from planning, is still "valiant in council." Achilles, whether he be standing or seated, is "swift-footed" or "fleet of foot," yet on the one occasion when he has the opportunity to show his fleetness of foot he was unable to overtake Hector. He must needs receive the help of Athena, who orders him to refresh himself while she induces Hector to come near. The simple fact that an epithet is applied to Achilles which has no interpretation in the events of the Iliad shows that he is a traditional hero and not a new creation of the poet. The epithet

[7]See Leaf, *Troy*, 159.

must have its explanation elsewhere. Odysseus early in the Iliad is called (B 278) "the city-sacking Odysseus," the reason for which is found not in the Iliad, but in outside tradition. Many other examples might be given, but these sufficiently illustrate the principle that in the Iliad certain epithets carry the implicit proof of traditions other than those told by the poet. If Hector be an old and traditional hero he should bring into the poem with him some traces of his earlier existence. In the Iliad there are twenty-seven various epithets applied to Hector—an unrivaled richness and variety of epithet—yet not one of these refers to any relationship, trait, or quality not shown in the poem itself. The Iliad furnishes a full explanation for every attribute given to Hector by Homer. If the number of epithets were small, this might be due to accident. Here, however, chance can have no part, and we may confidently assume that the tradition which among so many epithets has left no traces of its influence had no influence to leave, and that the character of Hector was beyond its power to shape or change.

As already stated, the Trojan leader, Paris, whom tradition furnished, was for moral reasons unworthy to be the great leader of either side. The poet was therefore obliged to substitute another whose human and moral excellencies fitted him for leadership. The degradation of Paris involved one great contradiction, namely, the impression that the warrior who did so much was a coward. The creation of Hector involved the second great contradiction, namely, the impression that the warrior who did so little was a mighty champion. Tradition narrowed the poet's range in either case. He might create a hero, but he did not create a war. The prowess of the Trojans is described only in vague expressions, since no Greek of independent importance is slain during the course of the Iliad. Patroclus is prominent merely because of his intimacy with Achilles, and besides him only two of any consequence fall, Medon, the bastard son of Ajax, the son of Oïleus, and the colorless Tlepolemus. On the Trojan side the slaughter is almost complete; Adrastus (the Greek names deserve notice), Asteropaeus, Dolon, Euphorbus, Hippothous, Cebriones, Lycaon, Socus, Coön, Pandarus, Sarpedon, and Hector, all perish. Paris is the only Trojan to wound a leader and then escape with his life. Evidently the strength of tradition tied Homer's hands and gave Paris a charmed life in the Iliad.

Hector receives high praise in general terms, but the events of the Iliad give no warrant for assigning him a high place as a soldier. He is found retreating at his first appearance in battle, is no match for Ajax in the duel, is almost slain by Diomede with a spear, and by Ajax with a rock, fainting each time; and he flies before Odysseus, Agamemnon, Patroclus, Diomede, Ajax, and Achilles. It is only as a man, a son, and a father

that Hector really wins respect; that is, just in
those qualities where he may appear noble without fighting the Greeks.

Why is Hector so great as a man, so secondary
as a soldier? If one will read the list of the
Trojans he will find, as already noted, that with
few exceptions they have Greek names; hence are
probably Greek adaptations or creations. The
Greeks had their own traditions of their own
leaders conducting a war against Troy to recover
Helen, who had been taken from Menelaus by
Paris. Paris bears a foreign name, his part in
tradition is sure; but tradition, so far as the Trojans were concerned, went little further. It did
not tell who built the ship, and so the poet had it
built by a Greek with a long line of Greek ancestors. The name Hector also has a good Greek
derivation and is surely Greek. It is doubtful if
the quarrel between Achilles and Agamemnon had
a larger place in the early Greek traditions of Troy
than the quarrel between Achilles and Odysseus,
which is given but ten verses in the eighth book of
the Odyssey (θ 73 ff.). At the opening of the Iliad
the Greeks are before Troy, and the Trojans
within the walls. The Greeks lose no leader,
warrior, or king of real importance. At the close
of the poem both sides are in the same relative
positions in which they were at the beginning.
On the Trojan side the slaughter has been almost
annihilation. Those who fell, Adrastus, Pandarus, Hector, and the rest, were for the most

part created to be participants in the events occasioned by the wrath of Achilles. They never had an existence elsewhere, and by their death the poet accounted for their absence from subsequent events of the epic tradition. This explains the contradictions in the character of Hector. The Greek leaders were already known and their fates determined. Tradition had decided that Ajax was to fall by his own hand, Achilles to be slain by Paris, Agamemnon by his wife and her paramour; the fate of each was already settled. What was there left for Hector? No new Greek general of outstanding importance could be added, and no local hero could be replaced, any more than a modern novel dealing with a modern war could add a new and important general to the list of famous heroes. Homer then was forced to make a Trojan champion without the privilege of allowing him to slay any one of the really great Greeks. Hector's greatness, therefore, is to be human and not military. Even so he must have some military glory, hence the poet created the character of Patroclus.

Patroclus does not appear in the Catalogue of the Ships, is not named in the *Cypria,* except under the influence of the Iliad, where it is said "Patroclus taking Lycaon to Lemnos sold him." Here the author of the *Cypria,* unable to explain the absence of Patroclus from tradition, reshapes the story of Lycaon as found in Homer, to give Patroclus a place in his poem. In the Iliad it

was Achilles and not Patroclus who sold Lycaon
(Φ 78). Evidently the author of the *Cypria*
changed the Iliad to secure a little glory for
Patroclus, in the same manner he gave to Hector
the honor of slaying Protesilaus. There were no
families claiming descent from Patroclus, and the
poet explains his lack of heroic following by the
simple device of having him slay one of his youthful companions, and then go into exile.

There was no place for Phoenix in a poem
which exalted Patroclus, since each owed his
prominence to the friendship of Achilles. The
creation of Hector involved the degradation of
Paris; the creation of Patroclus the practical
elimination of Phoenix. Homer, like an Athenian
father, could cause the death of no children but
his own; Patroclus he could expose, but tradition's child, Phoenix, he must not kill. So he
might slay Hector, and also, just because he was
the poet's own, he may have made him his mouth-
piece to express his own advanced ideas on religion, patriotism, and domestic relations. In
religion Hector is frankly rationalistic. He must
have shocked Homer's hearers, as he did the
scholiast, by his bold refusal to consider plain
omens (M 237), and must have voiced the poet's
patriotism when he told the Trojans the glory
which hallowed one who died in defense of his
fatherland. His ideals of domestic relations are
shown in the tenderness with which Hector treats
Andromache. It is certainly worthy of note that

this devoted husband should have been reared in a polygamous household and should himself have championed a war founded on treachery and adultery. In Hector the poet seems to have laid aside his mask and to show his own features.

The bitterness which Athena and Hera felt toward Hector followed him even after his death. They were both indignant at the mere suggestion that his corpse be spared the ignominy of being thrown to the dogs. This malignity cannot be explained by anything which has happened in the poem. The reason is that Hector was the champion in a war due to the scorning of their charms. He was hated not for his own sake but for his cause. Hector plays the part in the Iliad that Paris took in tradition, and just this fact, that he is substituting for Paris, explains their rage against him. The anger they felt for Paris must be spent on the one who assumed his place. This does not mean that the part taken by Hector in the scenes of the Iliad was ever taken by Paris, for none of these scenes existed before Homer. But in tradition it was Paris who was the leader of the Trojans, and it was against him that Hera and Athena were both enraged. With that tradition as a background, Homer created a new poem. The anger of Achilles was essentially the poet's own, the anger of these two goddesses against the Trojan leader he found as a definite part of the existing tradition. When, therefore, Homer created a new leader, that anger was an entailment on that leadership.

Milton stood in much the same relation to his sources as Homer stood to his. Milton must have an Adam, an Eve, a Garden of Eden, a Satan, a Tree of Forbidden Fruit; the tempter must appear in the form of a serpent and the woman must be the first to fall. All these the poet found in the Bible story and they must be retained. But the poetry, the descriptions, and most of the incidents were his own. Homer likewise had a list of Greek heroes, and a brief reference to the wrath of Achilles; he was familiar with the story of the rape of Helen by Paris, a prince of Troy. Tradition supplied him with scant information in regard to the Trojans, hence the long list of Trojans with Greek names. Although tradition told of the death of such first-class Greek heroes as Protesilaus, Palamedes, Achilles, and Ajax at Troy, it told of the death of none during the wrath of Achilles. Accordingly the poet had to content himself with the death of so subordinate a leader as Patroclus.

The Iliad is not the production of a poet who reshaped and refitted the work of others into a more perfect whole, who found his characters already made and retouched them now at this place, now at that, who added a little here and removed a little there. It is the work of a poet who largely created his own characters and gave them their names. Homer was the first poet to draw the portrait of Hector and to give him a name, a Greek common noun, and make it a proper noun, the name of a hero. How transparent most of the names given to Hector and his family, Astyanax, Deïphobus, Polydorus, Polites, Antiphonus, and Agathon! But the names of those heroes who undoubtedly belonged to tradition, names such as Peleus, Tydeus, Ajax, Icarius, and Bellerophon, do not so easily show their origin. Why are these names so dark while the names of Hector and his family are so transparent? The reason is this: the names of Hector and his brothers, except Paris, do not belong to tradition and are not traditional names. They are names put together by Homer himself. There may, indeed, be tradition in Homer, but it is only an incident; his real aim is poetry.

CHAPTER VIII

THE ILIAD AND THE ODYSSEY

We know nothing of Homer's sources or of the patterns which he followed—if he had any patterns to follow. Not a line, not a reliable reference to any piece of earlier literature has been preserved. There seems to be a possible allusion to the Argonautic expedition, but all the poems dealing with that adventure are much later than Homer, and may be based on inferences drawn from Homer rather than from earlier poetry. The tales of Meleager, of Nestor's young manhood, of the Amazons, and all the others may be susceptible of a similar interpretation.

There is thus only the scantiest material, and that doubtful, from which to reconstruct pre-Homeric poetry. And yet there must have been poets before Homer. The Iliad and the Odyssey show no experiments, no hesitancy in forcing a recalcitrant language into a difficult poetic meter. The grace and ease with which the words of Homer fall into dactylic rhythm could have come only after ages of poetic development. The meter makes use of a long and difficult verse, a verse which is far removed from the movement of primitive songs. Language so rich and so

complicated as Homer's contains within itself the
evidence of the heritage of many generations of
poets. It is doubtful if Milton's majestic verse was
more removed from the ordinary daily speech in
the time of Cromwell than the language of Homer
was from that of the common man in that early
day. The simple fact that there are five different forms for the infinitive "to be" (εἶναι, ἔμμεναι,
ἔμεναι, ἔμμεν, ἔμεν) and four forms for the simple
preposition "in" (ἐν, ἐνί, εἰν, εἰνί), all metrically
different, shows that the poet was not using the
language of the common people, but a language
of poetry in which these various forms had been
preserved.

A comparison of this language with any prose
rendering, however early and in whatever dialect,
will show its superlative poetic character. This
poetic cast can not be the work of a single man nor
the result of the wide use of poetic license. For
no people would permit the misuse or the mispro-
nunciation of their own language, yet they would
hear with delight old or poetic forms. Our own
use of rare and old words in poetry and in
devotion shows something akin to the poetic survivals in Homer.

All that we may in confidence say of the poets
who lived before Homer is that they provided him
with a language suited to the meter and to the
theme of his great poems. The interval between
the Iliad and the Odyssey cannot have been great,
if we may judge from their language and from

the civilization which both picture, and also from
the production of other great pieces of literature
in other ages and in other lands. Society is not
long content with any one style of excellence. The
enthusiasm which calls forth and rewards any one
species of genius is soon spent.

Had Homer lived at the end of the sixth
century, he would probably have been a lyric
poet; a generation later he would have been a
dramatist; and in the next generation he might
have been a writer of comedy, a philosopher, or
an orator. Aeschylus, who "was the first to raise
tragedy to the rank of real literature,"[1] was under
thirty years of age when Sophocles was born, and
with the death of Sophocles Greek tragedy had
run its creative course. State and religious support of the drama exerted a most conservative
influence, but despite this support the production
of Greek tragedies as real literature practically
coincided with the life of a single man, Sophocles.
In like manner old comedy, middle comedy, and
new comedy, each ran a brilliant and a brief
career; and the genealogies of Pherecydes, re-
puted to be the first man in Athens to apply prose
to the uses of literature, were separated by hardly
a generation from the history of Thucydides—
greatest of all histories.

It was not that men capable of writing lyric
poetry ceased to be born after the Persian Wars;
it was not that poets capable of dramatic efforts

[1] Flickinger, *The Greek Theater and Its Drama*, 2.

did not appear after the age of Pericles; it was because the tastes and the impulses of men were different. No one could imagine that Milton, were he now living, would turn his hand to a *Paradise Lost,* or Cervantes his to a *Don Quixote,* or that Dante would take up anew the problems of the *Inferno.* We have no knowledge of any people who could in two different centuries inspire kindred masterpieces of original genius. The period which could inspire short songs might last, but the influences which called into being long epic poems must certainly have been very brief.

The tradition that Homer and Hesiod once contested for the prize of poetic excellence, and that Hesiod won, is probably only another way of saying that the Greeks soon tired of the creative works of the imagination and preferred for a season the more practical descriptions of daily life, and the calm and unimaginative tales of theology. The utter collapse of the creative epic spirit as shown in the poetry of the Epic Cycle, if we base our opinion of the merits of these poems on the estimate of competent ancient authorities, shows that Homer had no successors. The Iliad and the Odyssey represent the golden age of epic poetry, and golden ages are always brief.

The Greeks at all times took great pride in authorship. Hesiod, the earliest poet after Homer, informs us that ''The Muses at one time taught Hesiod the gift of beautiful song,'' thus

enriching the world with his own name; Alcman
tells us that "Alcman composed these verses and
this song"; Theognis at the very beginning of
his poem says, "These verses are by Theognis
of Megara." Hecataeus, Herodotus, as well as
Thucydides, each begins his history with his own
name and an account of his own authorship.
Pheidias is said to have put his own likeness on
the shield which he made for the statue of Athena;
and similarly statues, votive tablets, and painted
vases were in classical times frequently marked
with the name of the artist and even with the
name of his father also and his home. This desire
for glory made it unnecessary to offer valuable
prizes at the great games—the ambition for personal renown was incentive enough. It was this
passion for personal glory that made each of the
Greek heroes at Salamis write his own name as
the one who had done the most to achieve that
victory. The Greeks in all these respects were
totally unlike their eastern neighbors, so that no
deductions in regard to oriental origins, except by
contrast, are of any value. The eminent Orien-
talist, Professor Jastrow, says:[2]

Authorship counted for little in the ancient Orient.
Greek culture with its emphasis on individualism may
be said to have invented the idea of authorship, so
far as it involves the individual's claim to his mental
product. We have no specific word for author in ancient
Hebrew, but merely a term ordinarily rendered as
"scribe," which may be used indifferently for a secre-

[2] Jastrow, M., *Hebrew and Babylonian Traditions*, 285.

tary who writes the dictation, for one who copies or compiles what another has composed, as well as for one who indites an original composition.

Another result of this method of literary production in the ancient Orient was that no book was produced at a single sitting, as it were. A book was always a compilation: it grew from age to age, much as a story grows with each repetition.

The Greeks lived in another world from this world of the Orient in which the "scribe" was simply the man who writes; in Greek the word poet means the creator, the man who produces something worth while. The very name shows the great honor in which the poet was held. Though the books of the Orient grew and changed from age to age, we know of no literary, no non-scientific, work of the Greeks which was not either finished by the author himself, or left permanently incomplete. Works of erudition or of philosophy may well have been preserved by pupils in the spirit in which these were received from the lips of the master, but this was not true of great literature. Thucydides died leaving his history incomplete and Xenophon undertook to tell the story of the Peloponnesian War for the period Thucydides left unfinished. But it was his own *Hellenica;* he did not try to add to or change what Thucydides had written.

The permanency of Greek traits makes it most unlikely that a poet who wrote the parting scene between Hector and Andromache, the speeches of the embassy, the ransoming of the body of

Hector, the journey of Telemachus, or the wanderings of Odysseus would have been willing to give up his own reputation for the glory of another, or that he would have reshaped the poetry already written by another so that he might successfully escape from the fame of his own great creations. Sir Philip Sidney's famous renunciation of the water he so feverishly craved was downright selfishness compared with the man who gave these great scenes of poetry to Homer and slipped stealthily away with such secrecy that his gift was unnoticed for nearly three thousand years. Sir Philip knew that at least two persons were conscious of his renunciation, the man who drank the water and the man who carried it, but the poet who gave all this glory to Homer had no such satisfaction—all he craved was to escape detection. And the man who did this was a self-conscious Greek!

The Iliad and the Odyssey were never anonymous, they were never quoted as the work of some unknown poet, and they were never assigned to any other poet than to Homer. The theory that the Iliad and the Odyssey are the anonymous creation of a long era, traditional poems produced by many bards in many ages, makes an appreciation of Greek civilization and Greek literature impossible, and confuses the Hebrew copying scribe with the exalted, creative Greek poet. Just this confusion, however, called into being Murray's *Rise of the Greek Epic*.

No poet ever put a higher estimate on his own poetry than Homer puts on the Iliad and the Odyssey. He says of Penelope that the glory of her excellence will never perish, that the gods will preserve her fame in pleasing song. Odysseus tells the Phaeacians that he is in the thoughts of all men and his glory has reached the skies. Helen consoles herself with the conviction that, after all, perhaps the Trojan war and all its woes were designed by Zeus that she and they who have suffered most may serve for a song among the generations yet unborn, and Alcinous, when he notices the emotions which Odysseus can not conceal whenever he hears the story of the woes endured by the Trojans and the Argives, tries to comfort him by saying: "Perhaps the gods have brought on these very woes and decreed destruction to men, that generations yet to be shall have the boon of song." Milton's muse

> That with no middle flight intends to soar
> Above the Aonian mount. . . . .

seems fairly self-conscious. But even Milton did not intimate that man lost the joys of Eden in order to gain the boon of immortality in the poetry of *Paradise Lost*.

It is not alone these actors whom I have named that look forward to the glory of song, but Agamemnon holds up before his men the disgrace which will be theirs in coming years, if they fail in the purpose of the war; Calchas tells of portents the renown of which shall never die, and

Hector, when he realizes that Athena has lured him to his doom, does not collapse but takes new courage in the determination to do some worthy deed, a deed to be known to future generations of men. A poet who could paint the sufferers from the war as repaid for it all by the immortality his song would bring to them could hardly have spurned a like immortality for himself.

This all-pervading, self-conscious, Greek individualism is no more evident in Pindar, who likens himself to the eagle, the divine bird of Zeus; or in Aeschylus, who unabashed by defeat in a dramatic contest proudly said, "I leave my merits to the decision of time," than it is in the epitaph of the sculptor: "I was an artist in stone, in no way inferior to Praxiteles," or in that of the woodchopper: "Here I lie a woodchopper; a better woodchopper I never saw." No man was ever more thoroughly a Greek than the creator of the Iliad and the Odyssey; he too must have had this Greek passion for individual glory.

The arguments against an historical Homer might seem justified by the fact that his name is not found in the writings of any Greek author until the middle of the sixth century, or presumably three hundred years after the time of the poet. (The conjectural reference to Homer by Callinus is based on an emendation and is most improbable.) This interval of three centuries seems a serious gap in the Homeric tradition. It must be remembered, however, that we have but little literature dating from the period between Homer and Xenophanes, who was the first to use the name of Homer. Also, this literature is highly fragmentary, largely preserved by grammarians and rhetoricians, who wished to illustrate some rule of language, or by compilers of books of choice quotations.

The first writers whose works are preserved in any large compass make frequent use of the name of the poet. Pindar and Simonides both quote him and use the name Homer, and in the first prose works which we have Homer's name frequently occurs. No one of these early writers refers to him as some unknown or shadowy personality, but as the writer whom everyone knew, and to whom Greece was most indebted for its theology and its civilization.

The first elegiac poet whose name we know is Callinus, who probably lived early in the seventh century. The first poet of the erotic elegy whose name we know is Mimnermus, who also lived in the seventh century. Oddly enough, however, the name of neither of these is found in any Greek writer before Strabo, whose life extended into the first century of the Christian era. That is, neither Callinus nor Mimnermus is named in any Greek literature for about seven hundred years after his own age, a period probably twice as long as from Homer to the first mention of his name. Yet those critics who have been most skeptical in regard to Homer do not throw the existence of Callinus and Mimnermus into the realm of the impossible or the improbable. How absolutely fallacious arguments from silence are likely to be is shown by the fact that the name of Chaucer is found neither in the poetry of Milton nor in that of Shakespeare, although the bulk of their poetry is far greater than all the poetry surviving from Homer to Pindar.

Although it is hard to decide how much in his plots or in his narratives Homer owed to the poets before him, there are certain traits or features which must have been his own. These are found in both poems, but not elsewhere, so far as we can judge, except in writings directly influenced by Homer.

The poet in selecting a war-theme for his Iliad did not take up the whole war, but a small fragment of that war just before its close, hence all the story of the Iliad covers hardly more than seven weeks, and the fighting is confined to but four days.[3] Twenty-one days are given to the opening book of the poem, and a like number to the closing book, nearly all of which pass by eventless. For instance, in the first book it is said that the plague lasted for nine days; and in the last book it is said that nine days were spent in preparing the pyre for Hector.

In the Odyssey Homer took a tale of wanderings and adventures which might have spread

[3] An excellent discussion is given by Professor Bassett in his article, ''The Structural Similarity of the Iliad and Odyssey, as Revealed in the Treatment of the Hero's Fate,'' *Class. Jour.*, XIV, 557.

over many years, but he confined his subject to the story of the last few days, so that the entire action of the Odyssey embraces about forty days, seventeen of which go by in a single verse which says that he sailed on for seventeen days, and in another verse it is said that he made his raft in four days, thus eliminating four days more, hence the days about which something is really told number less than twenty, or not far from the number of eventful days in the Iliad.

This superb piece of poetic economy of confining the action to a few important days seems to have been found in none of the poems of the Epic Cycle, if we may trust the authority of Aristotle, who contrasts the Iliad and the Odyssey in this regard with all the other epics. It is not found in any of the later Greek epic poets, such as Hesiod, Apollonius of Rhodes, and Quintus of Smyrna, nor in Vergil, whose poem covers the events of years. Vergil clearly followed the annalistic style of the poets of the Cycle rather than the method of the Iliad and the Odyssey. And it is not found in the *Paradise Lost* of Milton.

The first word of the Iliad is "wrath," $\mu\hat{\eta}\nu\iota\nu$, the first word of the Odyssey is "man," $\check{\alpha}\nu\delta\rho\alpha$, each poem thus giving the theme with the very first word. The story of the Iliad does not depend on the character of Achilles, but on his anger, an anger which eliminates even the hero from long stretches of the poem. But in the Odyssey the hero himself is always the center of the poem, quite as important when absent as when present.

Apparently Homer was the only poet of the early epic thus clearly to define his theme at the very start. The first verse of the *Thebais* is quoted as: "Sing of Argos, goddess, of thirsty Argos, whence the chieftains came." The *Thebais* seems to have been only remotely concerned with Argos itself; the real story was connected with the struggle at Thebes. The *Little Iliad* is said to have begun with the verse: "I sing of Ilium and Dardania of fine steeds." If we had no other means than this verse of judging the contents of that poem, we could hardly arrive at any idea of the varied themes given in the summary of Proclus. Each of the longer poems of Hesiod begins with praise of the Muses and gives no hint of the subject of the proposed poems. Apollonius of Rhodes introduces his *Argonautica* with the verse: "Beginning with thee, O Phoebus, I will call to mind the deeds of ancient men." This gives not the slightest inkling of the heroes or their exploits. Quintus of Smyrna begins with the verse "When god-like Hector was slain by the son of Peleus," leaving us quite in the dark in regard to his intended theme. All these introductions, or most of them, seem to be influenced by Homer, yet are totally unlike him. Horace, in his *Ars Poetica* 137, contrasts the simple dignified words in which Homer begins his poems with the bombastic introduction of the cyclic poem: *Fortunam Priami cantabo et nobile bellum.* It must have been more than pure accident that the

Iliad and the Odyssey both have this perfect introduction, a perfection approached by no other early
poet. Vergil's *Arma virumque cano,* and Milton's
Of man's first disobedience are simply imitations
of Homer.

In each poem Homer gives the impression that
the plot is well known. Nevertheless, so full are
the details, so clear the outlines, that he seems
in each to be creating a new plot and telling a
new story. We learn as if by accident the cause
of the anger, its intensity, and its results, and yet
we fully understand it without the help of any
details not given in the Iliad itself. In a like manner we learn that Odysseus has been twenty years
from home, that his wife is Penelope, that she is
beset with suitors, and that their land and home
have both drifted into something resembling anarchy. It is highly important in estimating the
small debt Homer owed to tradition that we are
able to appreciate both poems without any foot-
notes, and without any knowledge of the tradition
back of Homer, except as the poet himself gives
us that knowledge.

The most inattentive reader of Homer has
noticed how dramatic the story is and how large
a part is devoted to the speeches of the various
participants. We judge of the character of the
different actors in Homer, for the most part, not
from what the poet tells us, but from the words
of these men themselves. A little over one half
of the Iliad and the Odyssey is in direct speech.

The poetry of Homer is so dramatic, that, with very little editing, large parts of it could be put upon the stage almost in the very words of the original. The Odyssey shows no decline in the matter of direct speech, indeed a trifle less than one half of the Iliad, a little more than one half of the Odyssey, are composed in the form of direct speech.

No other ancient epic poet approached Homer in this regard, even when he had the example of Homer before him and tried to imitate him.[4] Hesiod has few or no speaking characters and they most unimportant; and the scanty fragments from the Epic Cycle seem to warrant the assumption that these poems were narrative rather than dramatic. It must have been due to the genius of Homer that his characters reveal their natures by their own words and acts rather than by any description by the poet himself. This assumption applies to no single portion but to all parts of both poems. Even in the last book of the Odyssey, which the critics despise, these character-revealing speeches abound.

Both poems describe things of superlative excellence, not in themselves, but in the effect they produce upon others. When Helen first appeared Homer made no attempt to audit her charms. We know how beautiful she must have been from the words spoken by the old men of Troy, men long

---

[4] The figures are given by Elderkin, ''Aspect of the Speech in the Later Greek Epic,'' Johns Hopkins University dissertation, 1906.

beyond the years of youthful enthusiasm, when they said: "The Greeks and the Trojans cannot be blamed for undergoing sorrows these many years for a woman so beautiful." We have an added feeling for the majesty of Agamemnon when we hear Priam say, as he looks down from the walls of Troy: "I never saw so stately or so handsome a man, for he surely looks like a king." The words are all the more convincing, since Priam is ignorant of the fact that he was asking about Agamemnon.

In the last book of the Iliad, when Priam came into the tent or hut of Achilles to beg the body of his son, the poet brought Priam, the father of the man who had slain Achilles' nearest friend, into the presence of the very warrior who had robbed him of Hector as well as of other sons, and thus described their feelings as they gazed, each into the face of his foe: "Then Priam the son of Dardanus looked with surprise at Achilles, because of his stature and his beauty, for his face was as the face of the gods; while Achilles in his turn stood astonished when he saw the majestic presence and heard the noble language of Priam." Where have dignity and nobility ever been better pictured than in these verses? The fact that Priam should see nobility and beauty in his greatest foe is praise indeed, and that Achilles should gaze wrapped in admiration at the majestic presence of the very man whose son he had determined to throw to the dogs gives an impression of exalted beauty beyond all description.

When Telemachus and Peisistratus, the son of Nestor, came to visit Menelaus in his own magnificent palace, the palace is not described, but we catch some glimpses of its beauty from these words: "And they gazed with wonder throughout the palace of the Zeus-nourished Menelaus, for it was as the splendor of the sun or moon throughout the high-roofed halls."

The island of Calypso must have been of wondrous beauty, for Hermes, when he came straight from splendid Olympus to warn that goddess that she could no longer detain Odysseus, even Hermes "stood and looked with rapture at the beauties of the island." It was only after he had feasted his eyes on this earthly paradise that he continued on his mission. What must have been the charm of an island that could thus hold a god familiar with the beauties of Olympus! It adds impressiveness to the devotion Odysseus had for his own native land when we know that he preferred all the struggles and dangers which lay between him and Ithaca rather than quietly to live in that entrancing island.

We get some indication of the extreme ugliness of the monstrous wife of the cannibal Antiphates from the simple verse: "The men when they saw her looked on her with loathing."

Such a superlative piece of poetic economy, describing unusual objects by their effect, is, naturally, rarely used; and Homer has numerous detailed descriptions—such as the descriptions of the shield of Agamemnon, the chariot and horses of Poseidon, the ugliness of Thersites, the palace and gardens of Alcinous, the cave of the Cyclops, or the hideousness of Scylla.

Homer loved to withhold the crisis and also to prolong the suspense in cases of great excitement. When Achilles comes back with his new armor we expect that he will rush upon the field and immediately meet and slay Hector, but Odysseus interferes with the demand that the soldiers first be fed, a suggestion which leads to debate and delay. When at last all impediments seem removed and Achilles rushes forward to avenge Patroclus, a multitude of actions postpone the climax. The hero must first meet Aeneas, and then Lycaon; he must be thwarted by the god of the river; and even then it is only after another series of delays that he comes face to face with Hector. Exactly similar is the plan of the Odyssey. When that hero returns to his palace and sees with his own eyes the violence of the suitors, we expect that he will at once assert his power and take vengeance. But there is first the fight with the beggar, the washing of the feet, the story of the scar, the description of the bow and how he came by it, then the attempts to string it, and the seemingly interminable series of delays; and then at last the vengeance.

Both poems agree so closely in the multiplicity of events and in the withholding of the climax, that almost the same number of events intervene between the time when Achilles hears of the death of Patroclus and determines to avenge the death of his friend, and the slaying of Hector, as intervene between the return of Odysseus to his own palace and the slaughter of the suitors. This great retardation in each poem covers about twenty-two hundred verses. This is no happy accident, no chance coincidence, and it is no imitation. It shows in the two poems the creative impulse of one and the same mind.

Homer loves also in moments of great excitement to prolong the suspense. Achilles, when he sees that the Trojans are on the point of burning the fleet, smites his thighs in intense excitement and urges Patroclus to rush forth and save the ships, knowing that if they are consumed neither he nor the Greeks can escape. Just at this moment of haste and anxiety the poet stops to tell us how Patroclus arms himself. With aggravating minuteness he describes each piece of the armor and gives a list of all the officers in the army, with their ancestry. He tells how Achilles goes to his tent and gets a cup his mother had given him, how he purifies it, and washes it in fresh water, then washes his own hands and offers a prayer of sixteen verses, after which he calmly returns to his tent and carefully puts the cup back in the chest. In exactly one hundred and fifty verses after Achilles smote his thighs does the poet permit Patroclus to move to the rescue.

In the Odyssey when the hero, clinging under the belly of the ram, is carried from the cave of the Cyclops, the monster lays hold of the ram and makes him a long speech, while we and Odysseus are alike in suspense. Again, when Odysseus comes to his palace in the guise of a beggar, he makes his plans for vengeance revolve around his ability to keep himself unknown to the members of his household. But while his feet are being washed by the aged Eurycleia, who had nursed him in his infancy, she recognizes the old scar, and just when we are in intense anxiety to know whether she will baffle his plans, now that she knows the beggar is none other than the long absent Odysseus, the poet lets us wait while he tells of the birth and babyhood of the hero, how he came to be named Odysseus, how he happened to visit his grandfather, the details of the hunt on one of those visits, and all about the wild boar that made the scar, the scar which the nurse so easily recognized.

But, though the poet may leave us anxious in regard to details, he always keeps us informed, well in advance, of the outcome of the plot and its chief features. No one needs to turn to the last page to see how matters are to end. When Agamemnon prays that the sun may not set until he has slain Hector and destroyed Troy, we are told that this prayer is not to be answered. We are warned that the plans to bring the war to an end by means of a duel between Paris and

Menelaus are to be abortive. We are told in advance that Patroclus' interest in the welfare of the Greeks is to lead to his own ruin; that the ships will not be destroyed by fire; that Hector will be slain; and that his body will not be thrown to the dogs. No hearer of the Iliad is ever in doubt regarding the final outcome of every important scene. In the Odyssey likewise we are assured that the hero will return in twenty years; that he will have lost all his companions; that he will escape from the Cyclops, the Sirens, Charybdis, Scylla, and the wrath of Poseidon; that he will slay the suitors, find his wife faithful, and will once more reëstablish his rightful power in Ithaca.

By thus forecasting events the poet relieved the anxiety of the hearers in regard to the final outcome. Neither poem, however, loses its power or sustained interest from the fact that the fate of the hero is never in doubt. Rather, as in the work of the Athenian dramatists, the merit of the poet lies in the manner of telling a story the main issues of which are already known to the audience. The simple fact that the poet of the Iliad and the Odyssey felt it necessary to point out in advance the course of the story, and that he did not assume that it was already known, is a strong indication that the plot was not the gift of tradition, but the independent creation of the poet himself.

The climax of each poem comes not at the end, but in the twenty-second book. The climax of the Iliad is the death of Hector; that of the Odyssey, the death of the suitors. The Iliad does not close until a pyre has been erected for Patroclus and funeral games held in his honor; not until the body of Hector has been ransomed and he, as well as Patroclus, has been given the honor of funeral dirges and a dignified burial. The Iliad, which has seen so much bloodshed, so much excitement, and so much passion, ends with the calm and simple verses: "And having heaped for him a mound, they returned homeward, and being assembled within the palace of Priam they feasted with bounteous repast. Thus then they buried Hector, the knight." In the Odyssey the palace is cleansed and purified after the slaughter of the suitors, and the guilty servants punished. Penelope recognizes that the beggar is indeed her husband, Odysseus, who gives her a brief outline of his adventures. The shades of the suitors are conducted to Hades, where many of the Greek leaders of the Trojan war are seen again; Odysseus then goes to the farm, where he meets and comforts his father; the factions of Ithaca are reconciled; and this poem, with all its trials, sorrows, and cruelties ends with these quiet verses: "Thus spake Athena, and Odysseus rejoiced in his heart, while Pallas Athena ratified friendly oaths between all factions, Pallas Athena, the daughter of Aegis-bearing Zeus, as she appeared

like unto Mentor both in form and in voice.'' The
similarity of the closing of both of these poems
is startling, yet there is nothing of imitation.
Both carry the marks of the same creative power
working to the same end under different, although
kindred conditions.

The action of each poem is initiated by the
gods. Athena gives Achilles the cue for his
anger, arouses Odysseus to stop the panic of the
Greeks, provides the Iliad with a new start by
encouraging Pandarus to break the oath, and is
the means through which Hector succumbs to
Achilles. It is Athena also who puts the action
of the Odyssey in motion, and finds a setting for
the tale of the wanderings of Odysseus by her
advice to Nausicaa. She encourages and aids
Odysseus in his slaughter of the suitors, just as
she had cared for Achilles in the pursuit of
Hector. The gods furnished the solution for the
difficult problem of rescuing the body of Hector
from a revengeful Achilles exactly as they solved
the problem of bringing peace to Ithaca after the
slaughter of so many of its nobility at the hands
of the king. In each poem the gods are burlesqued
and made the subject of coarse mirth, and in each
they are used to give the air of probability to
things which in themselves are most improbable.

The opening of each poem is in a measure
repeated or reproduced in the close. In the first
book of the Iliad the plague lasts for nine days,
the gods visit the Aethiopians for twelve days,

and Achilles nourishes his anger. On the twenty-
first day the gods return, and Thetis goes to
Olympus that she may supplicate Zeus to honor
her son. These numbers are repeated in the last
book of the Iliad so closely that not only does this
book cover twenty-one days, but the days are
divided into nine and twelve precisely as they are
in book one. Here, too, Achilles spends a like
number of days in anger, here he is again visited
by his mother, and she again goes to Olympus
to consult with Zeus. The Iliad opens in the presence of the hosts of the Achaeans, and closes in
the presence of the hosts of the Trojans. There
is thus a balance not only in time and in action,
but in the setting as well.

In the Odyssey, also, each scene in the introduction corresponds with a like scene in the close.
The poem is set in motion by the agency of Athena,
it is brought to an end by the same goddess. In
the beginning she hurries to Ithaca with the permission of Zeus in order to arouse Telemachus
to action, and at the close by the command of that
same god she hastens back to Ithaca bringing
peace to the island. Nearly every actor is named
or present in the first book, and nearly all reappear to make their final bow at the close. The
suitors are dead, but they are represented by their
kinsmen.

It was the sense of harmony or of balance
which led the poet to open the Iliad with a period
covering twenty-one days and to close it with the

same number. A like feeling in the Odyssey made him give one day to the opening and one to the closing of that poem. This balance can hardly be due to chance, but to the poetic instinct of a single mind.

No one feature of Homeric poetry so impresses the casual reader as the large number of repeated verses. No other work of classical literature furnishes a parallel. But, in this regard, no part of the poetry of Homer differs from any other part. Each poem, both as a whole and in its parts, consists of repeated verses aggregating about one third of the entire number. Even those books which the critics characterize as *centos,* patchwork, made up of verses mechanically taken from other parts of the poems, are no more marked by repeated verses than are other books' which are regarded as pure and original. The book most censured for its repeated verses is the last book of the Odyssey. This book, however, with its 548 verses, has only 180 repeated verses, or just a trifle under the average for all of Homer. The total number of verses in Homer is 27,853. Of these 9253 are repeated verses, that is, thirty-three per cent of the entire number are repeated, which is, as already said, just a shade higher than the percentage in the last book of the Odyssey. Whatever may be our feeling in regard to repeated verses, the Iliad and the Odyssey clearly reflect the same poetic attitude in this matter.

Lastly, and most important, these two poems are of almost the same length. Each was divided by scholars into twenty-four books, the books of the Odyssey averaging a trifle over five hundred verses each, while those of the Iliad are a little under six hundred and sixty. No poem of classical Greece can be compared as to length with either the Iliad or the Odyssey. No poem antedating comparatively late times has been preserved, except the Homeric poems, which contains as many as two thousand verses. The longest extant lyric poem is an epic theme treated in lyric style by Pindar and it has but two hundred and ninety-nine verses. The longest single drama of which we have any knowledge is the *Oedipus at Colonus*, with seventeen hundred and eighty verses.

We cannot do more than make a rough guess of the size of the different poems of the epic cycle. The *Thebais* is said to have contained about six thousand[5] verses, and the *Epigoni* was of about the same length, that is, each was hardly one-half the size of the Odyssey. The *Cypria* had eleven books, the *Aethiopis* five, the *Destruction of Troy* two, the *Little Iliad* four, and the *Nosti* five. Thus the poem which told of the return of the various Achaeans had less than a fourth as many books as the poem which told of the return of the single hero, Odysseus, while the *Telegoneia* had but two books. We are not permitted to be dogmatic

[5] Müller, *History of Ancient Greek Literature*, 71, says 5600 verses.

about the size of each of these books, but we can
hardly be mistaken when we believe that no one
of these poems could have approached the length
of either of the Homeric poems.

It seems clear also that the mass or bulk of
these poems grew less the later they originated.
The *Telegoneia,* written about 600 B.C., had but
two books, but even two books made a long poem
for that time, since the seventh and the sixth
centuries were the centuries of short songs. The
great names in literature during that period are
Archilochus, Alcman, Ibycus, Sappho, Alcaeus,
Solon, Tyrtaeus, and Stesichorus. At the turn
into the fifth century the great names are Pindar,
Anacreon, Simonides, and Bacchylides. No one
of these seems to have produced songs or poems
of more than modest compass.

If any one will run over the list of famous
poets who came just before, during, and immediately after the time of Peisistratus, he must
notice that this was the era of short songs. This
was also the age of the Seven Wise Men who
gained fame by the brevity of their speech. Yet
this era of the short song and the pithy speech is
the very time in which Wolf and his followers,
down to the last article just written by Bethe,
assume that a commission gathered scattered
songs into one or two gigantic poems.

It is not merely an accident that Sappho and
Alcaeus wrote lyric poetry at the same time, and
that Pindar, Simonides, Anacreon, Ibycus, and

Bacchylides were almost contemporaries. Nor is it an accident that Aeschylus, Sophocles, and Euripides in the next century were all dramatists. All of these were the children of their own age, and nothing could be more improbable than that an age which inspired and produced short songs should have created by commission or otherwise two poems of such bulk as the Iliad and the Odyssey. The tendency was all the other way. Stesichorus even broke up the masses of the epic into lyric songs, and Terpander a little earlier set small portions of Homer to the music of the lyre. We may be sure that it was not a lyric age nor a dramatic age but an age wholly given over to the epic that called forth these two lengthy poems.

Matthew Arnold named Homer the poet of the grand style, but he is also the poet of the grand outlines, the massive scale. Everything is presented on such a huge canvas. Not a Trojan acts until verse 1419 of the Iliad, and even though it is a war poem no less than 2400 verses precede the first shedding of blood. The Odyssey is the story of Odysseus, but that hero does not appear until well along in the fifth book. Everything is so deliberate and sketched in such large outlines. It is this massive scale on which both poems are constructed that makes impossible the theory that they could have been built out of smaller songs. One might make a huge pile of sand by putting together many little piles of sand, but one cannot give the appearance of an oak to any mass of twigs, however numerous. The size of an organism is as evident in the parts as in the whole, and the vast scale on which the Iliad and the Odyssey are constructed is as manifest in the single books as in the entire poem. An annalistic poem might have one hundred thousand verses, yet be constructed on a small scale, the bulk simply depending on the many small events, as a dictionary expands by the simple addition of new names. This great bulk of the Homeric poems is not due to diffusiveness or idle words, and Matthew Arnold picks out as one of the essential marks of Homeric poetry its rapidity and directness.

This massive structure is unlike anything else produced by the Greeks and is absolutely foreign to the poetic impulses of the sixth century, that is, to the age of Peisistratus.

This massiveness is not in the length of the poems so much as in the broad framework on which the parts are built. Vergil wrote a poem which sang both of a man and of arms, that is, he took both the Iliad and the Odyssey for his theme and he had Homer before him, yet the Aeneid is six thousand verses shorter than the single poem, the Iliad. Nothing in Homer so fills me with wonder as this huge reach and grasp. It is not so much the size of the poems as the massiveness of the details which reveals the power and the greatness of the poet, and in this the Iliad and the Odyssey stand alone, but exactly alike. It is possible to believe that Greece had one man who could project such mighty, such enormous, works of art, but it is unthinkable that she had at any period two men or a group of men with any such capacity.

Everything fits into the theory of a single Homer: the civilization, the language, the gods, the outlines, the marks of genius; and all these are supported by the unanimous verdict of the best poets and the greatest critics of twenty-five hundred years.

The evidence for the unity of the Iliad and the Odyssey is so strong that we should be compelled to postulate a single Homer even if ancient Greece had believed in many. But antiquity was united in the belief of one divine Homer, and only one.

CORRIGENDA

Page 51, line 18, *for* This small island, *read* A military
contingent from this small island.

Page 137, line 15, *for* these same two travellers, *read* the
two young travellers.

Page 191, line 21. The suggestion to make the wrestling
match a sham came from Ajax.

Page 214, line 8, *for* he follows her to, *read* he remained
with her at.

INDEX

Abstract nouns, use of, in Iliad and Odyssey, 85–88.

Achilleis, the *Ur-Ilias* theory regarding, 83–105.

Actors, The, in Homer, introduction of, 166–171, 223; individualization of, 172; traditions concerning, 196, 224, 225, 229, 234, 235, 237–239; names of, 225–226; epithets applied to, 231–232.

Aelian, 14, 25, 38.

Aeneid, 1. *See also* Vergil.

Aeolic forms, in Iliad and Odyssey, 4, 96.

Aeschines, 29.

Aeschylus, 27, 197, 198, 199, 242, 248, 267.

Aethiopis, 11, 265.

Ajax and the Athenians, bearing of relations of, on the Homeric Question, 47–51.

Alcaeus, 266.

Alcman, 244, 266.

Alexandria, 7, 155.

Allen, 32, 33, 36, 72.

Amphictyonic Council, 62.

Anacreon, 266.

Anonymity of authorship of Iliad and Odyssey, 246.

Antigonus of Carystus, *Paradoxes*, evidence for Homeric authorship of Thebais, 21.

Antimachus, 16, 59.

Antiphon, 24.

Apollonius of Rhodes, 180, 252.

Archaeology, testimony of, 135. *See also* Mycenae; Troy; etc.

Archilochus, 266.

Argos, and the Argives, 18–20; inscription to Homer, 19.

Aristarchus, 24, 40, 41, 50, 151.

Aristophanes, 15, 28.

Aristotle, 14–15, 34, 37, 38, 49, 56, 64, 77, 251.

Armor, 117–118.

Arnold, Matthew, 74, 202, 267, 268.

Astronomy, testimony of, 107–109.

Athenaeus, 14, 28, 71.

Athens (Attica), City Dionysia in, 45; influence on Homeric poetry, 47–55, 55–72; direct references to, in Odyssey, 51–52; geography of, not familiar to Homer, 53. *See also* Peisistratus.

Authorship, Greek pride in, 243.

Bacchylides, 266, 267.

Bards (rhapsodes, reciters), Homeric, 7, 61, 64, 219; regulations concerning, 65–66; Homer's use of, in Iliad and Odyssey, 128–134; manner of Homeric recitation, 156–160.

Bassett, 101, 118, 250.

Bekker, cited, 96.

Bentley, cited, 66, 69, 71.

Bergk, cited on contradictions in Homer, 145–147.

Bethe, cited, 79, 80, 81, 121, 123, 147, 220.

Bolling, cited, 86, 87.

Bunyan, 173.

Byron, 173.

Callimachus, 33.

Callinus, 15, 16, 248, 249.

Case-endings, use of, in Iliad and Odyssey, 92–93.

Catalogue of the Ships, 47, 48.

Cauer, cited, 86.